100
VERSES
EVERY
MOM
NEEDS
TO KNOW

The quoted ideas expressed in this book (but not Scripture verses) are not, in all cases, exact quotations, as some have been edited for clarity and brevity. In all cases, the author has attempted to maintain the speaker's original intent. In some cases, quoted material for this book was obtained from secondary sources, primarily print media. While every effort was made to ensure the accuracy of these sources, the accuracy cannot be guaranteed. For additions, deletions, corrections, or clarifications in future editions of this text, please write Freeman-Smith, LLC.

The Holy Bible, King James Version

The Holy Bible, New King James Version (NKJV) Copyright © 1982 by Thomas Nelson, Inc. Used by permission.

New Century Version®. (NCV) Copyright © 1987, 1988, 1991 by Word Publishing, a division of Thomas Nelson, Inc. All rights reserved. Used by permission.

The Holman Christian Standard Bible™ (Holman CSB) Copyright © 1999, 2000, 2001 by Holman Bible Publishers. Used by permission.

The Holy Bible, New International Version®. (NIV) Copyright © 1973, 1978, 1984 International Bible Society. Used by permission of Zondervan. All rights reserved.

The Holy Bible. New Living Translation (NLT) copyright © 1996 Tyndale Charitable Trust. Used by permission of Tyndale House Publishers.

The New American Standard Bible®, (NASB) Copyright © 1960, 1962, 1963, 1968, 1971, 1972, 1973, 1975, 1977, 1995 by The Lockman Foundation. Used by permission.

Scripture taken from The Message. (MSG) Copyright © 1993, 1994, 1995, 1996, 2000, 2001, 2002. Used by permission of NavPress Publishing Group.

Cover Design by Kim Russell / Wahoo Designs
Page Layout by Bart Dawson

ISBN 978-1-60587-113-4

Printed in the United States of America

100
VERSES
EVERY
MOM
NEEDS
TO KNOW

TABLE OF CONTENTS

Introduction   9

Verse 1. John 3:16   10
Verse 2. Psalm 118:24   13
Verse 3. Genesis 1:1-3   16
Verse 4. Matthew 6:9-13   19
Verse 5. Psalm 23:1-3   22
Verse 6. 2 Peter 3:18   25
Verse 7. John 15:9   28
Verse 8. Matthew 23:11-12   31
Verse 9. John 15:11   34
Verse 10. Philippians 4:4   37
Verse 11. Luke 6:37   40
Verse 12. Matthew 25:40   43
Verse 13. Philippians 4:8   46
Verse 14. John 12:46   49
Verse 15. Psalm 127:1   52
Verse 16. Matthew 5:7   55
Verse 17. Proverbs 22:24-25   58
Verse 18. Matthew 19:26   61

Verse 19. Psalm 100:1-2   64

Verse 20. 1 John 4:11   67

Verse 21. Psalm 30:5   70

Verse 22. Matthew 22:37-38   73

Verse 23. 1 Chronicles 28:20   76

Verse 24. Psalm 145:8-9   79

Verse 25. Psalm 1:1-2   82

Verse 26. Psalm 23:4   85

Verse 27. Isaiah 40:31   88

Verse 28. Psalm 46:10   91

Verse 29. 1 Corinthians 13:13   94

Verse 30. Matthew 6:33-34   97

Verse 31. Proverbs 3:5-6   100

Verse 32. John 15:5   103

Verse 33. Matthew 7:7-8   106

Verse 34. Exodus 20:3   109

Verse 35. John 10:10   112

Verse 36. Joshua 24:15   115

Verse 37. Ephesians 2:8-9   118

Verse 38. James 1:19-20   121

Verse 39. Matthew 7:12   124

Verse 40. Psalm 55:22   127

Verse 41. Psalm 16:11   130

Verse 42. 1 John 2:3   133

Verse 43. 2 Timothy 3:16-17   136

Verse 44. Ecclesiastes 3:1   139

Verse 45. Proverbs 4:23   142

Verse 46. Luke 9:23-24   145

Verse 47. Psalm 46:1   148

Verse 48. Matthew 6:24   151

Verse 49. 1 Corinthians 13:4-7   154

Verse 50. Matthew 17:20   157

Verse 51. Matthew 24:35   160

Verse 52. Matthew 28:19-20   163

Verse 53. 1 Corinthians 10:31   166

Verse 54. 1 Samuel 16:7   169

Verse 55. Proverbs 17:9   172

Verse 56. Proverbs 27:12   175

Verse 57. Deuteronomy 30:19-20   178

Verse 58. 1 Peter 5:8   181

Verse 59. 1 Thessalonians 5:16-18   184

Verse 60. Galatians 5:22-23   187

Verse 61. Proverbs 22:6   190

Verse 62. 1 Corinthians 13:11   193

Verse 63. 1 Peter 5:2   196

Verse 64. Ephesians 4:31-32   199

Verse 65. Isaiah 41:10   202

Verse 66. Proverbs 10:9   205

Verse 67. Philippians 3:13-14   208

Verse 68. 1 Peter 1:13   211

Verse 69. John 15:26   214

Verse 70. Luke 24:1-6   217

Verse 71. Proverbs 25:11   220

Verse 72. Proverbs 28:13   223

Verse 73. Proverbs 16:3   226

Verse 74. 1 Corinthians 15:33   229

Verse 75. Matthew 25:20-21   232

Verse 76. Proverbs 16:18   235

Verse 77. 1 John 1:9   238

Verse 78. 1 Timothy 4:12   241

Verse 79. 1 Timothy 6:6-8   244

Verse 80. James 4:8   247

Verse 81. Proverbs 22:7   250

Verse 82. 2 Chronicles 31:21   253

Verse 83. 2 Thessalonians 3:10   256

Verse 84. 2 Corinthians 5:17   259

Verse 85. Psalm 106:1   262

Verse 86. 1 Corinthians 10:13   265

Verse 87. 2 Corinthians 9:6-7   268

Verse 88. Job 2:10   271

Verse 89. James 1:22   274

Verse 90. Matthew 19:6   277

Verse 91. Matthew 5:6   280

Verse 92. 1 Peter 5:6-7   283

Verse 93. James 2:17   286

Verse 94. Psalm 90:12   289

Verse 95. Proverbs 16:16   292

Verse 96. John 8:32   295

Verse 97. 1 John 2:15   298

Verse 98. Malachi 3:6   301

Verse 99. Matthew 5:14-16   304

Verse 100. Psalm 122:1   307

Tips for Memorizing Bible Verses   310

INTRODUCTION

The counsel of the LORD standeth for ever,
the thoughts of his heart to all generations.
Psalm 33:11 KJV

There are some Bible verses that are so important, so crucial to faith and family, that every mother should know them by heart. So here's a question for you, Mom: can you focus on just 100 of these verses? Of course you can; of course you should; and this book can help.

This text examines 100 of the most familiar verses from God's Holy Word. These verses, which you've probably heard many times before, are short enough, and memorable enough, for you to place safely in your long-term mental database. So do yourself and your loved ones a favor: study each verse and do your best to place it permanently in your mind and in your heart. When you do, you'll discover that having God's Word in your heart is even better than having a Bible on your bookshelf.

VERSE 1

For God so loved the world,
that he gave his only begotten Son,
that whosoever believeth in him should not perish,
but have everlasting life.

John 3:16 KJV

THE GIFT OF ETERNAL LIFE

We begin with John 3:16, a verse that you've undoubtedly known since childhood. After all, this verse is, quite possibly, the most widely recognized sentence in the entire Bible. But even if you memorized this verse many years ago, you still need to make sure it's a verse that you can recite by heart.

Eternal life is not an event that begins when we die. Eternal life begins when we invite Jesus into our hearts. The moment we allow Jesus to reign over our hearts, we've already begun our eternal journeys.

As a thoughtful Christian parent, it's important to remind your child that God's plans are not limited to the ups and downs of everyday life. In fact, the ups and downs of the daily grind are, quite often, impossible for us to understand. As mere mortals, our understanding of the present and our visions for the future—like our lives here on earth—are limited. God's vision is not burdened by such limitations: His plans extend throughout all eternity. And we must trust Him even when we cannot understand the particular details of His plan.

So let us praise the Creator for His priceless gift, and let us share the Good News with all who cross our paths. We return our Father's love by accepting His grace and by sharing His message and His love. When we do, we are blessed here on earth and throughout all eternity.

MORE THOUGHTS ABOUT ETERNAL LIFE

I can still hardly believe it. I, with shriveled, bent fingers, atrophied muscles, gnarled knees, and no feeling from the shoulders down, will one day have a new body— light, bright and clothed in righteousness—powerful and dazzling.

Joni Eareckson Tada

God has promised us abundance, peace, and eternal life. These treasures are ours for the asking; all we must do is claim them. One of the great mysteries of life is why on earth do so many of us wait so very long to lay claim to God's gifts.

Marie T. Freeman

Like a shadow declining swiftly . . . away . . . like the dew of the morning gone with the heat of the day; like the wind in the treetops, like a wave of the sea, so are our lives on earth when seen in light of eternity.

Ruth Bell Graham

Your choice to either receive or reject the Lord Jesus Christ will determine where you spend eternity.

Anne Graham Lotz

If you are a believer, your judgment will not determine your eternal destiny. Christ's finished work on Calvary was applied to you the moment you accepted Christ as Savior.

Beth Moore

The damage done to us on this earth will never find its way into that safe city. We can relax, we can rest, and though some of us can hardly imagine it, we can prepare to feel safe and secure for all of eternity.

Bill Hybels

A WORD TO THE WISE

Remind your child that the appropriate moment to let Jesus rule one's heart is always the present moment.

VERSE 2

This is the day which the LORD hath made;
we will rejoice and be glad in it.
Psalm 118:24 KJV

CELEBRATE THE GIFT OF LIFE

Today is a non-renewable resource—once it's gone, it's gone forever. Our responsibility, as thoughtful believers, is to use this day in the service of God's will and in the service of His people. When we do so, we enrich our own lives and the lives of those whom we love.

God has richly blessed us, and He wants you to rejoice in His gifts. That's why this day—and each day that follows—should be a time of prayer and celebration as we consider the Good News of God's free gift: salvation through Jesus Christ.

Oswald Chambers correctly observed, "Joy is the great note all throughout the Bible." E. Stanley Jones echoed that thought when he wrote "Christ and joy go together." But, even the most dedicated Christians can, on occasion, forget to celebrate each day for what it is: a priceless gift from God.

What do you expect from the day ahead? Are you expecting God to do wonderful things, or are you living beneath a cloud of apprehension and doubt? The familiar words of Psalm 118:24 remind us that every day is a cause for celebration. Our duty, as believers, is to rejoice in God's marvelous creation.

Today, celebrate the life that God has given you. Today, Mom, put a smile on your face, kind words on your lips, and a song in your heart. Be generous with your praise and free with your encouragement. And then, when you have celebrated life to the full, invite your friends to do likewise. After all, this is God's day, and He has given us clear instructions for its use. We are commanded to rejoice and be glad. So, with no further ado, let the celebration begin . . .

MORE THOUGHTS ABOUT JOYFUL LIVING

If you can forgive the person you were, accept the person you are, and believe in the person you will become, you are headed for joy. So celebrate your life.

Barbara Johnson

Today is mine. Tomorrow is none of my business. If I peer anxiously into the fog of the future, I will strain my spiritual eyes so that I will not see clearly what is required of me now.

Elisabeth Elliot

When the dream of our heart is one that God has planted there, a strange happiness flows into us. At that moment, all of the spiritual resources of the universe are released to help us. Our praying is then at one with the will of God and becomes a channel for the Creator's purposes for us and our world.

Catherine Marshall

Submit each day to God, knowing that He is God over all your tomorrows.

Kay Arthur

Christ is the secret, the source, the substance, the center, and the circumference of all true and lasting gladness.

Mrs. Charles E. Cowman

As Christians, we must live a day at a time. No person, no matter how wealthy or gifted, can live two days at a time. God provides for us day by day.

Warren Wiersbe

A WORD TO THE WISE

Today is a wonderful, one-of-a-kind gift from God. Treat it that way.

VERSE 3

In the beginning God created the heavens
and the earth. The earth was without form,
and void; and darkness was on the face of the deep.
And the Spirit of God was hovering over
the face of the waters. Then God said,
"Let there be light"; and there was light.

Genesis 1:1-3 NKJV

CELEBRATING GOD'S CREATION

I n the beginning, God created everything: the things we see and the things we don't. And each morning, the sun rises upon a glorious world that is a physical manifestation of God's infinite power and His infinite love. And yet, because of the incessant demands of everyday life, we're sometimes too busy to notice.

We live in a society filled with more distractions than we can possibly count and more obligations than we can possibly meet. Is it any wonder, then, that we often overlook God's handiwork as we rush from place to place, giving scarcely a single thought to the beauty that surrounds us?

Today, take time to really observe the world around you. Take time to offer a prayer of thanks for the sky above and the beauty that lies beneath it. And take time to ponder the miracle of God's creation. The time you spend celebrating God's wonderful world is always time well spent.

Man was created by God to know
and love Him in a permanent,
personal relationship.

Anne Graham Lotz

MORE THOUGHTS ABOUT GOD'S CREATION

How awesome that the "Word" that was in the beginning, by which and through which God created everything, was—and is—a living Person with a mind, will, emotions, and intellect.

Anne Graham Lotz

God expresses His love through creation.

Charles Stanley

No philosophical theory which I have yet come across is a radical improvement on the words of Genesis, that "in the beginning God made Heaven and Earth."

C. S. Lewis

Can't follow the stars? Follow the One who made them.

Anonymous

Because God created the Natural—invented it out of His love and artistry—it demands our reverence.

C. S. Lewis

A WORD TO THE WISE

Every day can be a celebration of God's creation. And every day should be.

VERSE 4

After this manner therefore pray ye:
Our Father which art in heaven,
Hallowed be thy name. Thy kingdom come.
Thy will be done in earth, as it is in heaven.
Give us this day our daily bread.
And forgive us our debts, as we forgive our debtors.
And lead us not into temptation,
but deliver us from evil:
For thine is the kingdom, and the power,
and the glory, for ever. Amen

Matthew 6:9-13 KJV

THE LORD'S PRAYER

"**O**ur Father which art in heaven, hallowed be thy name." These familiar words begin the Lord's Prayer, a prayer that you've heard on countless occasions. It's the prayer that Jesus taught His followers to pray, and it's a prayer that you probably know by heart.

You already know what the prayer says, but have you thought carefully, and in detail, about exactly what those words mean? Hopefully so. After all, this simple prayer was authored by the Savior of mankind.

Today, take the time to carefully consider each word in this beautiful passage. When you weave the Lord's Prayer into the fabric of your life, you'll soon discover that God's Word and God's Son have the power to change everything, including you.

MORE THOUGHTS ABOUT GOD

I lived with Indians who made pots out of clay which they used for cooking. Nobody was interested in the pot. Everybody was interested in what was inside. The same clay taken out of the same riverbed, always made in the same design, nothing special about it. Well, I'm a clay pot, and let me not forget it. But, the excellency of the power is of God and not us.

Elisabeth Elliot

God has put into each of our lives a void that cannot be filled by the world. We may leave God or put Him on hold, but He is always there, patiently waiting for us . . . to turn back to Him.

Emilie Barnes

God is the beyond in the midst of our life.

Dietrich Bonhoeffer

God is not a supernatural interferer; God is the everlasting portion of his people. When a man born from above begins his new life, he meets God at every turn, hears him in every sound, sleeps at his feet, and wakes to find him there.

Oswald Chambers

When all else is gone, God is left, and nothing changes Him.

Hannah Whitall Smith

A sense of deity is inscribed on every heart.

John Calvin

God is an infinite circle whose center is everywhere and whose circumference is nowhere.

St. Augustine

A WORD TO THE WISE

If your kids can recite the Lord's Prayer by heart, congratulations. If they can't, then what are you waiting for?

VERSE 5

The Lord is my shepherd; I shall not want.
He makes me to lie down in green pastures;
He leads me beside the still waters.
He restores my soul.

Psalm 23:1-3 NKJV

GOD'S PROTECTION

David, the author of the 23rd Psalm, realized that God was his shield, his protector, and his salvation. And if we're wise, we realize it, too. After all, God has promised to protect us, and He intends to keep His promise.

In a world filled with dangers and temptations, God is the ultimate armor. In a world filled with misleading messages, God's Word is the ultimate truth. In a world filled with more frustrations than we can count, God's Son offers the ultimate peace.

Will you accept God's peace and wear God's armor against the dangers of our world? Hopefully so—because when you do, you can live courageously, knowing that you possess the supreme protection: God's unfailing love for you.

The world offers no safety nets, but God does. He sent His only begotten Son to offer you the priceless gift of eternal life. And now you are challenged to return God's love by obeying His commandments and honoring His Son.

Sometimes, in the crush of everyday life, God may seem far away, but He is not. God is everywhere you have ever been and everywhere you will ever go. He is with you night and day; He knows your thoughts and your prayers. And, when you earnestly seek His protection, you will find it because He is here—always—waiting patiently for you to reach out to Him. And the next move, of course, is yours.

God will never let you sink
under your circumstances.
He always provides a safety net
and His love always encircles.

Barbara Johnson

MORE THOUGHTS ABOUT GOD'S PROTECTION

He goes before us, follows behind us, and hems us safe inside the realm of His protection.

Beth Moore

The Lord God of heaven and earth, the Almighty Creator of all things, He who holds the universe in His hand as though it were a very little thing, He is your Shepherd, and He has charged Himself with the care and keeping of you, as a shepherd is charged with the care and keeping of his sheep.

Hannah Whitall Smith

Our responsibility is to feed from Him, to stay close to Him, to follow Him—because sheep easily go astray—so that we eternally experience the protection and companionship of our Great Shepherd the Lord Jesus Christ.

Franklin Graham

A WORD TO THE WISE

Earthly security is an illusion. Your only real security comes from the loving heart of God.

VERSE 6

But grow in the grace and knowledge
of our Lord and Savior Jesus Christ.
To Him be the glory both now and forever.

2 Peter 3:18 NKJV

SPIRITUAL GROWTH

The words of 2 Peter 3:18 make it clear: spiritual growth is a journey, not a destination. When it comes to your faith, God doesn't intend for you to stand still. He wants you to keep moving and growing. In fact, God's plan for you includes a lifetime of prayer, praise, and spiritual growth.

Many of life's most important lessons are painful to learn. During times of heartbreak and hardship, we must be courageous and we must be patient, knowing that in His own time, God will heal us if we invite Him into our hearts.

Spiritual growth need not take place only in times of adversity. We must seek to grow in our knowledge and love of the Lord every day that we live. In those quiet moments when we open our hearts to God, the One who made us keeps remaking us. He gives us direction, perspective, wisdom, and courage. The appropriate moment to accept those spiritual gifts is the present one.

Are you as mature as you're ever going to be? Hopefully not! When it comes to your faith, God doesn't intend for you to become "fully grown," at least not in this lifetime. In fact, God still has important lessons that He intends to teach you. So ask yourself this: what lesson is God trying to teach me today? And then go about the business of learning it.

MORE THOUGHTS ABOUT SPIRITUAL GROWTH

If all struggles and sufferings were eliminated, the spirit would no more reach maturity than would the child.

Elisabeth Elliot

We look at our burdens and heavy loads, and we shrink from them. But, if we lift them and bind them about our hearts, they become wings, and on them we can rise and soar toward God.

Mrs. Charles E. Cowman

We set our eyes on the finish line, forgetting the past, and straining toward the mark of spiritual maturity and fruitfulness.

Vonette Bright

Grow, dear friends, but grow, I beseech you, in God's way, which is the only true way.

Hannah Whitall Smith

You are either becoming more like Christ every day or you're becoming less like Him. There is no neutral position in the Lord.

Stormie Omartian

We often become mentally and spiritually barren because we're so busy.

Franklin Graham

The vigor of our spiritual lives will be in exact proportion to the place held by the Bible in our lives and in our thoughts.

George Mueller

A WORD TO THE WISE

No matter what your level of spiritual maturity, you can always grow. Show your children the way to know God better: daily devotions; prayer; worship; and witnessing.

As the Father loved Me,
I also have loved you; abide in My love.
John 15:9 NKJV

CHRIST'S LOVE

How much does Christ love us? More than we, as mere mortals, can comprehend. His love is perfect and steadfast. Even though we are fallible and wayward, the Good Shepherd cares for us still. Even though we have fallen far short of the Father's commandments, Christ loves us with a power and depth that are beyond our understanding. The sacrifice that Jesus made upon the cross was made for each of us, and His love endures to the edge of eternity and beyond.

Hannah Whitall Smith spoke to believers of every generation when she advised, "Keep your face upturned to Christ as the flowers do to the sun. Look, and your soul shall live and grow." How true. When we turn our hearts to Jesus, we receive His blessings, His peace, and His grace.

Christ is the ultimate Savior of mankind and the personal Savior of those who believe in Him. As His servants, we should place Him at the very center of our lives. And, every day that God gives us breath, we should share Christ's love and His message with a world that needs both.

Christ's love changes everything. When you accept His gift of grace, you are transformed, not only for today, but also for all eternity. If you haven't already done so, accept Jesus Christ as your personal Savior. He's waiting patiently for you to invite Him into your heart. Please don't make Him wait a single minute longer.

MORE THOUGHTS ABOUT CHRIST'S LOVE

To God be the glory, great things He has done; / So loved He the world that He gave us His Son.

Fanny Crosby

Live your lives in love, the same sort of love which Christ gives us, and which He perfectly expressed when He gave Himself as a sacrifice to God.

Corrie ten Boom

Sometimes Agape really hurts. It broke the heart of God to demonstrate His love to us through Christ but its ultimate end was salvation.

Beth Moore

This hard place in which you perhaps find yourself is the very place in which God is giving you opportunity to look only to Him, to spend time in prayer, and to learn long-suffering, gentleness, meekness—in short, to learn the depths of the love that Christ Himself has poured out on all of us.

Elisabeth Elliot

Jesus loves me! This I know, for the Bible tells me so. Little ones to him belong; they are weak, but he is strong. / Yes, Jesus loves me! Yes, Jesus loves me! Yes, Jesus loves me! The Bible tells me so.

Anna B. Warner and Susan Warner

No man ever loved like Jesus. He taught the blind to see and the dumb to speak. He died on the cross to save us. He bore our sins. And now God says, "Because He did, I can forgive you."

Billy Graham

A WORD TO THE WISE

Jesus loves you. His love can—and should—be the cornerstone and the touchstone of your life.

VERSE 8

The greatest among you must be a servant.
But those who exalt themselves will be humbled,
and those who humble themselves will be exalted.

Matthew 23:11-12 NKJV

STAYING HUMBLE

A s fallible human beings, we have so much to be humble about. Why, then, is humility such a difficult trait for us to master? Precisely because we are fallible human beings. Yet if we are to grow and mature as Christians, we must strive to give credit where credit is due, starting, of course, with God and His only begotten Son.

As Christians, we have been refashioned and saved by Jesus Christ, and that salvation came not because of our own good works but because of God's grace. Thus, we are not "self-made"; we are "God-made," and we are "Christ-saved." How, then, can we be boastful? The answer, of course, is that, if we are honest with ourselves and with our God, we simply can't be boastful . . . we must, instead, be eternally grateful and exceedingly humble. Humility, however, is not easy for most of us. All too often, we are tempted to stick out our chests and say, "Look at me; look what I did!" But, in the quiet moments when we search the depths of our own hearts, we know better. Whatever "it" is, God did that. And He deserves the credit.

We are never stronger than
the moment we admit we are weak.

Beth Moore

MORE THOUGHTS ABOUT HUMILITY

If you know who you are in Christ, your personal ego is not an issue.

Beth Moore

That's what I love about serving God. In His eyes, there are no little people . . . because there are no big people. We are all on the same playing field. We all start at square one. No one has it better than the other, or possesses unfair advantage.

Joni Eareckson Tada

All kindness and good deeds, we must keep silent. The result will be an inner reservoir of personality power.

Catherine Marshall

I can usually sense that a leading is from the Holy Spirit when it calls me to humble myself, to serve somebody, to encourage somebody, or to give something away. Very rarely will the evil one lead us to do those kind of things.

Bill Hybels

A WORD TO THE WISE

You must remain humble or face the consequences. Pride does go before the fall, but humility often prevents the fall.

VERSE 9

These things have I spoken unto you,
that my joy might remain in you,
and that your joy might be full.

John 15:11 KJV

MAKING HIS JOY YOUR JOY

Christ made it clear: He intends that His joy should become our joy. Yet sometimes, amid the inevitable hustle and bustle of life here on earth, we can forfeit—albeit temporarily—the joy of Christ as we wrestle with the challenges of daily living.

Jonathan Edwards, the 18th-century American clergyman, observed, "Christ is not only a remedy for your weariness and trouble, but He will give you an abundance of the contrary: joy and delight. They who come to Christ do not only come to a resting-place after they have been wandering in a wilderness, but they come to a banqueting-house where they may rest, and where they may feast. They may cease from their former troubles and toils, and they may enter upon a course of delights and spiritual joys."

If, today, your heart is heavy, open the door of your soul to Christ. He will give you peace and joy. And, if you already have the joy of Christ in your heart, share it freely, just as Christ freely shared His joy with you.

God knows everything.
He can manage everything, and He loves us.
Surely this is enough for
a fullness of joy that is beyond words.
Hannah Whitall Smith

MORE THOUGHTS ABOUT JOY

The Christian lifestyle is not one of legalistic do's and don'ts, but one that is positive, attractive, and joyful.

Vonette Bright

A life of intimacy with God is characterized by joy.

Oswald Chambers

Joy is the heart's harmonious response to the Lord's song of love.

A. W. Tozer

Our sense of joy, satisfaction, and fulfillment in life increases, no matter what the circumstances, if we are in the center of God's will.

Billy Graham

God gives to us a heavenly gift called joy, radically different in quality from any natural joy.

Elisabeth Elliot

A WORD TO THE WISE

Every day, God gives you many reasons to rejoice. The rest is up to you.

VERSE 10

Rejoice in the Lord always.
Again I will say, rejoice!
Philippians 4:4 NKJV

REJOICE!

A re you living a life of agitation, consternation, or celebration? If you're a believer, it should most certainly be the latter. With Christ as your Savior, every day should be a time of celebration.

Oswald Chambers correctly observed, "Joy is the great note all throughout the Bible." C. S. Lewis echoed that thought when he wrote, "Joy is the serious business of heaven." But, even the most dedicated Christians can, on occasion, forget to celebrate each day for what it is: a priceless gift from God.

Today, celebrate the life that God has given you. Today, put a smile on your face, kind words on your lips, and a song in your heart. Be generous with your praise and free with your encouragement. And then, when you have celebrated life to the full, invite your friends to do likewise. After all, this is God's day, and He has given us clear instructions for its use. We are commanded to rejoice and be glad. So, with no further ado, Mom, let the celebration begin . . .

If you can forgive the person you were,
accept the person you are,
and believe in the person you will become,
you are headed for joy.
So celebrate your life.

Barbara Johnson

MORE THOUGHTS ABOUT CELEBRATION

According to Jesus, it is God's will that His children be filled with the joy of life.

Catherine Marshall

Christ is the secret, the source, the substance, the center, and the circumference of all true and lasting gladness.

Mrs. Charles E. Cowman

Joy is a by-product not of happy circumstances, education or talent, but of a healthy relationship with God and a determination to love Him no matter what.

Barbara Johnson

Joy is the direct result of having God's perspective on our daily lives and the effect of loving our Lord enough to obey His commands and trust His promises.

Bill Bright

A WORD TO THE WISE

Cheerfulness is contagious: Remember that a cheerful family starts with cheerful parents.

Do not judge, and you will not be judged.
Do not condemn, and you will not be condemned.
Forgive, and you will be forgiven.

Luke 6:37 Holman CSB

FORGIVENESS: YES, JUDGING: NO

Even the most devoted Christians may fall prey to a powerful yet subtle temptation: the temptation to judge others. But as Christians, we are commanded to refrain from such behavior. The warning of Luke 6:37 is clear: "Do not judge." Yet, as fallible, imperfect human beings living in a stressful world, we are sorely tempted to do otherwise.

As Jesus came upon a young woman who had been condemned by the Pharisees, He spoke not only to the crowd that was gathered there, but also to all generations when He warned, "He that is without sin among you, let him first cast a stone at her" (John 8:7 KJV). Christ's message is clear, and it applies not only to the Pharisees of ancient times, but also to us.

We have all fallen short of God's commandments, and none of us, therefore, are qualified to "cast the first stone."

Thankfully, God has forgiven us, and we, too, must forgive others. As Christian believers, we are warned that to judge others is to invite fearful consequences: to the extent we judge others, so, too, will we be judged by God. Let us refrain, then, from judging our neighbors. Instead, let us forgive them and love them in the same way that God has forgiven us.

Christians think they are
prosecuting attorneys or judges,
when, in reality,
God has called all of us to be witnesses.

Warren Wiersbe

MORE THOUGHTS ABOUT JUDGING OTHERS

Judging draws the judgment of others.

Catherine Marshall

Don't judge other people more harshly than you want God to judge you.

Marie T. Freeman

An individual Christian may see fit to give up all sorts of things for special reasons—marriage, or meat, or beer, or cinema; but the moment he starts saying these things are bad in themselves, or looking down his nose at other people who do use them, he has taken the wrong turn.

C. S. Lewis

Being critical of others, including God, is one way we try to avoid facing and judging our own sins.

Warren Wiersbe

A WORD TO THE WISE

To the extent you judge others, so, too, will you be judged. So you must, to the best of your ability, refrain from judgmental thoughts and words.

VERSE 12

Assuredly, I say to you,
inasmuch as you did it to one of the least of these
My brethren, you did it to Me.

Matthew 25:40 NKJV

GENEROSITY NOW

In the busyness and confusion of daily life, it is easy to lose focus, and it is easy to become frustrated. We are imperfect human beings struggling to manage our lives as best we can, but we often fall short. When we are distracted or disappointed, we may neglect to share a kind word or a kind deed. This oversight hurts others, but it hurts us most of all.

Matthew 25:40 warns, "Inasmuch as you did it to one of the least of these My brethren, you did it to Me." When we extend the hand of friendship to those who need it most, God promises His blessings. When we ignore the needs of others—or mistreat them—we risk God's retribution.

Today, Mom, slow yourself down and be alert for those who need your smile, your kind words, or your helping hand. Make kindness a centerpiece of your dealings with others. They will be blessed, and you will be, too. When you spread a heaping helping of encouragement and hope to the world, you can't help getting a little bit on yourself.

MORE THOUGHTS ABOUT KINDNESS

When we do little acts of kindness that make life more bearable for someone else, we are walking in love as the Bible commands us.

Barbara Johnson

It is one of the most beautiful compensations of life that no one can sincerely try to help another without helping herself.

Barbara Johnson

When we Christians are too busy to care for each other, we're simply too busy for our own good . . . and for God's.

Marie T. Freeman

Do all the good you can. By all the means you can. In all the ways you can. In all the places you can. At all the times you can. To all the people you can. As long as you can.

John Wesley

The mark of a Christian is that he will walk the second mile and turn the other cheek. A wise man or woman gives the extra effort, all for the glory of the Lord Jesus Christ.

John Maxwell

Be so preoccupied with good will that you haven't room for ill will.

E. Stanley Jones

Scientists tell us that every word and picture ever broadcast electronically is still somewhere out in space, billions of miles away. If humans ever go to other planets, they may see an old episode of Gunsmoke. Amazing as that sounds, there is something even more astonishing: Not a single act of goodness in Jesus' name has ever disappeared. Every act of kindness reaches out and touches the lives of thousands of people—one at a time.

Dennis Swanberg

A little kindly advice is better than a great deal of scolding.

Fanny Crosby

A WORD TO THE WISE

Your children will learn how to treat others by watching you (not by listening to you!). Acts of kindness speak louder than words.

*Finally, brethren, whatever things are true,
whatever things are noble, whatever things are
just, whatever things are pure, whatever things are
lovely, whatever things are of good report, if there is
any virtue and if there is anything praiseworthy—
meditate on these things.*

Philippians 4:8 NKJV

THE DIRECTION OF
YOUR THOUGHTS

How will you direct your thoughts today? Will you obey the words of Philippians 4:8 by dwelling upon those things that are true, noble, and just? Or will you allow your thoughts to be hijacked by the negativity that seems to dominate our troubled world?

Are you fearful, angry, bored, or worried? Are you so preoccupied with the concerns of this day that you fail to thank God for the promise of eternity? Are you confused, bitter, or pessimistic? If so, God wants to have a little talk with you.

God intends that you be an ambassador for Him, an enthusiastic, hope-filled Christian. But God won't force you to adopt a positive attitude. It's up to you to think positively about your blessings and opportunities . . . or not. So, today and every day hereafter, celebrate this life that God has given you by focusing your thoughts and your energies upon "things that are excellent and worthy of praise." Today, count your blessings instead of your hardships. And thank the Giver of all things good for gifts that are simply too numerous to count.

Attitude is the mind's paintbrush;
it can color any situation.

Barbara Johnson

MORE THOUGHTS ABOUT YOUR THOUGHTS

Preoccupy my thoughts with your praise beginning today.

Joni Eareckson Tada

As we have by faith said no to sin, so we should by faith say yes to God and set our minds on things above, where Christ is seated in the heavenlies.

Vonette Bright

The things we think are the things that feed our souls. If we think on pure and lovely things, we shall grow pure and lovely like them; and the converse is equally true.

Hannah Whitall Smith

It is the thoughts and intents of the heart that shape a person's life.

John Eldredge

A WORD TO THE WISE

Kids are amazingly intuitive. Believe it or not, your child is probably a mind reader. If your kid is like most kids, he or she is surprisingly sensitive. So do yourself and your child a favor: be careful with your thoughts as well as your actions.

VERSE 14

*I have come as a light into the world,
that whoever believes in Me
should not abide in darkness.*

John 12:46 NKJV

JESUS IS THE LIGHT

The words of John 12:46 teach us that Jesus is the light of the world. And, John 14:6-7 instructs us that Jesus is, "the way, the truth, and the life." Without Christ, we are as far removed from salvation as the east is removed from the west. And without Christ, we can never know the ultimate truth: God's truth.

Truth is God's way: He commands His believers to live in truth, and He rewards those who do so. Jesus is the personification of God's liberating truth, a truth that offers salvation to mankind.

Do you seek to walk with God? Do you seek to feel His presence and His peace? Then you must walk in truth; you must walk in the light; you must walk with the Savior. There is simply no other way.

When you can't see Him,
trust Him.
Jesus is closer
than you ever dreamed.

—

Max Lucado

MORE THOUGHTS ABOUT JESUS

I am truly happy with Jesus Christ. I couldn't live without Him. When my life gets beyond the ability to cope, He takes over.

Ruth Bell Graham

There was One, who for "us sinners and our salvation," left the glories of heaven and sojourned upon this earth in weariness and woe, amid those who hated Him and finally took His life.

Lottie Moon

In your greatest weakness, turn to your greatest strength, Jesus, and hear Him say, "My grace is sufficient for you, for My strength is made perfect in weakness" (2 Corinthians 12:9, NKJV).

Lisa Whelchel

When we are in a situation where Jesus is all we have, we soon discover He is all we really need.

Gigi Graham Tchividjian

A WORD TO THE WISE

You are a light upon the world around you. Make sure that your light is both bright and good.

VERSE 15

Unless the Lord builds a house,
its builders labor over it in vain;
unless the Lord watches over a city,
the watchman stays alert in vain.

Psalm 127:1 Holman CSB

HE WATCHES OVER US

Have you ever faced challenges that seemed too big to handle? Have you ever faced big problems that, despite your best efforts, simply could not be solved? If so, you know how uncomfortable it is to feel helpless in the face of difficult circumstances. Thankfully, even when there's nowhere else to turn, you can turn your thoughts and prayers to God, and He will respond.

God's hand uplifts those who turn their hearts and prayers to Him. Count yourself among that number. When you do, you can live courageously and joyfully, knowing that "this too will pass"—but that God's love for you will not. And you can draw strength from the knowledge that you are a marvelous creation, loved, protected, and uplifted by the ever-present hand of God.

MORE THOUGHTS ABOUT GOD'S PROTECTION

In all the old castles of England, there was a place called the keep. It was always the strongest and best protected place in the castle, and in it were hidden all who were weak and helpless and unable to defend themselves in times of danger. Shall we be afraid to hide ourselves in the keeping power of our Divine Keeper, who neither slumbers nor sleeps, and who has promised to preserve our going out and our coming in, from this time forth and even forever more?

Hannah Whitall Smith

The task ahead of us is never as great as the Power behind us.

Anonymous

Trials are not enemies of faith but opportunities to reveal God's faithfulness.

Barbara Johnson

Gather the riches of God's promises which can strengthen you in the time when there will be no freedom.

Corrie ten Boom

There is no safer place to live than the center of His will.

Calvin Miller

Through all of the crises of life—and we all are going to experience them—we have this magnificent Anchor.

Franklin Graham

God delights in spreading His protective wings and enfolding His frightened, weary, beaten-down, worn-out children.

Bill Hybels

Our future may look fearfully intimidating, yet we can look up to the Engineer of the Universe, confident that nothing escapes His attention or slips out of the control of those strong hands.

Elisabeth Elliot

When you fall and skin your knees and skin your heart, He'll pick you up.

Charles Stanley

A WORD TO THE WISE

When you are in the center of God's will, you are in the center of God's protection.

VERSE 16

*Blessed are the merciful,
because they will be shown mercy.*

Matthew 5:7 Holman CSB

BE MERCIFUL

If we wish to build lasting relationships, we must learn how to forgive. Why? Because our loved ones are imperfect (as are we). How often must we forgive our spouses and our friends? More times than we can count; to do otherwise is to disobey God.

Are you easily frustrated by the inevitable imperfections of others? Are you easily angered? Do you sometimes hold on to feelings of bitterness and regret? If so, perhaps you need a refresher course in the art of forgiveness.

Perhaps granting forgiveness is hard for you. If so, you are not alone. Genuine, lasting forgiveness is often difficult to achieve—difficult but not impossible. Thankfully, with God's help, all things are possible, and that includes forgiveness. But even though God is willing to help, He expects you to do some of the work.

If there exists even one person, alive or dead, whom you have not forgiven (and that includes yourself and, of course, your spouse), follow God's commandment and His will for your life: forgive. Bitterness, anger, and regret are not part of God's plan for your life. Forgiveness is.

God expects us to forgive others
as He has forgiven us;
we are to follow His example
by having a forgiving heart.

Vonette Bright

MORE THOUGHTS ABOUT LOVE AND FORGIVENESS

The fact is, God no longer deals with us in judgment but in mercy. If people got what they deserved, this old planet would have ripped apart at the seams centuries ago. Praise God that because of His great love "we are not consumed, for his compassions never fail" (Lam. 3:22).

Joni Eareckson Tada

When God forgives, He forgets. He buries our sins in the sea and puts a sign on the shore saying, "No Fishing Allowed."

Corrie ten Boom

The more you practice the art of forgiving, the quicker you'll master the art of living.

Marie T. Freeman

Forgiveness is the precondition of love.

Catherine Marshall

A WORD TO THE WISE

You should love all people, including your enemies. It's a difficult job, but with God's help, you can do it.

VERSE 17

Make no friendship with an angry man,
and with a furious man do not go,
lest you learn his ways
and set a snare for your soul.

Proverbs 22:24-25 NKJV

DEALING WITH
DIFFICULT PEOPLE

Face it: sometimes people can be difficult to deal with . . . very, very difficult. When other people are unkind to you, you may be tempted to strike back, either verbally or in some other way. Resist that temptation. Instead, remember that God corrects other people's behaviors in His own way, and He doesn't need your help (even if you're totally convinced that He does).

So when other people behave cruelly, foolishly, or impulsively—as they will from time to time—don't respond in kind. Instead, speak up for yourself as politely as you can, and walk away. Then, forgive everybody as quickly as you can and leave the rest up to God.

MORE THOUGHTS ABOUT DIFFICULT PEOPLE

When something robs you of your peace of mind, ask yourself if it is worth the energy you are expending on it. If not, then put it out of your mind in an act of discipline. Every time the thought of "it" returns, refuse it.

Kay Arthur

You can be sure you are abiding in Christ if you are able to have a Christlike love toward the people that irritate you the most.

Vonette Bright

A pessimist is someone who believes that when her cup runneth over she'll need a mop.

Barbara Johnson

Discouraged people, if they must be discouraged, ought, at least, to keep their discouragements to themselves, hidden away in the privacy of their own bosoms lest they should discourage the hearts of their brethren.

Hannah Whitall Smith

If some hypocrites do intrude among us, it should not astonish us.

C. H. Spurgeon

A keen sense of humor helps us to overlook the unbecoming, understand the unconventional, tolerate the unpleasant, overcome the unexpected, and outlast the unbearable.

Billy Graham

Sour godliness is the devil's religion.

John Wesley

We are all fallen creatures and all very hard to live with.

C. S. Lewis

A WORD TO THE WISE

If you can't find it in your heart to forgive those who have hurt you, you're hurting yourself more than you're hurting anyone else. But remember: forgiveness should not be confused with enabling. Even after you've forgiven the difficult person in your life, you are not compelled to accept continued mistreatment from him or her.

VERSE 18

*But Jesus looked at them and said to them,
"With men this is impossible,
but with God all things are possible."*

Matthew 19:26 NKJV

WITH GOD,
ALL THINGS ARE POSSIBLE

Sometimes, because we are imperfect human beings with limited understanding and limited faith, we place limitations on God. But, God's power has no limitations. God will work miracles in our lives if we trust Him with everything we have and everything we are. When we do, we experience the miraculous results of His endless love and His awesome power.

Miracles, both great and small, are an integral part of everyday life, but usually, we are too busy or too cynical to notice God's handiwork. We don't expect to see miracles, so we simply overlook them.

Do you lack the faith that God can work miracles in your own life? If so, it's time to reconsider. If you have allowed yourself to become a "doubting Thomas," you are attempting to place limitations on a God who has none. Instead of doubting your Heavenly Father, you must trust Him. Then, you must wait and watch . . . because something miraculous is going to happen to you, and it might just happen today.

MORE THOUGHTS ABOUT MIRACLES

When we face an impossible situation, all self-reliance and self-confidence must melt away; we must be totally dependent on Him for the resources.

Anne Graham Lotz

There is Someone who makes possible what seems completely impossible.

Catherine Marshall

I could go through this day oblivious to the miracles all around me or I could tune in and "enjoy."

Gloria Gaither

Here lies the tremendous mystery—that God should be all-powerful, yet refuse to coerce. He summons us to cooperation. We are honored in being given the opportunity to participate in his good deeds. Remember how He asked for help in performing his miracles: Fill the water pots, stretch out your hand, distribute the loaves.

Elisabeth Elliot

Are you looking for a miracle? If you keep your eyes wide open and trust in God, you won't have to look very far.

Marie T. Freeman

I have been suspected of being what is called a fundamentalist. That is because I never regard any narrative as unhistorical simply on the ground that it includes the miraculous.

C. S. Lewis

Only God can move mountains, but faith and prayer can move God.

E. M. Bounds

The miracles in fact are a retelling in small letters of the very same story which is written across the whole world in letters too large for some of us to see.

C. S. Lewis

A WORD TO THE WISE

God is in the business of doing miraculous things. You should never be afraid to ask Him for a miracle.

Make a joyful noise unto the LORD,
all ye lands.
Serve the LORD with gladness:
come before his presence with singing.

Psalm 100:1-2 KJV

MAKE A JOYFUL NOISE

When is the best time to "make a joyful noise" by praising God? In church? Before dinner is served? When we tuck little children into bed? None of the above. The best time to praise God is all day, every day, to the greatest extent we can, with thanksgiving in our hearts, and with a song on our lips.

Too many of us, even well-intentioned believers, tend to compartmentalize our waking hours into a few familiar categories: work, rest, play, family time, and worship. To do so is a mistake. Worship and praise should be woven into the fabric of everything we do; it should never be relegated to a weekly three-hour visit to church on Sunday morning.

Theologian Wayne Oates once admitted, "Many of my prayers are made with my eyes open. You see, it seems I'm always praying about something, and it's not always convenient—or safe—to close my eyes." Dr. Oates understood that God always hears our prayers and that the relative position of our eyelids is of no concern to Him.

Today, Mom, find a little more time to lift your concerns to God in prayer, and praise Him for all that He has done. Whether your eyes are open or closed, He's listening.

When I met Christ,
I felt that I had swallowed sunshine.

E. Stanley Jones

MORE THOUGHTS ABOUT JOY

Where the soul is full of peace and joy, outward surroundings and circumstances are of comparatively little account.

Hannah Whitall Smiith

He wants us to have a faith that does not complain while waiting, but rejoices because we know our times are in His hands—nail-scarred hands that labor for our highest good.

Kay Arthur

Our God is so wonderfully good, and lovely, and blessed in every way that the mere fact of belonging to Him is enough for an untellable fullness of joy!

Hannah Whitall Smith

Gratitude changes the pangs of memory into a tranquil joy.

Dietrich Bonhoeffer

A WORD TO THE WISE

Joy begins with a choice—the choice to establish a genuine relationship with God and His Son. Joy does not depend upon your circumstances, but upon your relationship with God.

VERSE 20

Beloved, if God so loved us,
we also ought to love one another.

1 John 4:11 NKJV

LOVE ONE ANOTHER

Genuine love requires patience and perseverance. Sometimes we are sorely tempted to treat love as if it were a sprint (which it is not). Genuine love is always a marathon, and those who expect it to be otherwise will always be disappointed.

Building lasting relationships requires a steadfast determination to endure, and as an example of perfect perseverance, we need look no further than our Savior, Jesus Christ. Jesus finished what He began. Despite the torture He endured, despite the shame of the cross, Jesus was steadfast in His faithfulness to God. We, too, must remain faithful in our relationships, especially during times of transition or hardship.

The next time you are tempted to give up on a relationship, ask yourself this question: "What would our Savior do?" When you find the answer to that question, you will know precisely what you should do.

For love to be true,
it sometimes has to be velvet
and sometimes it has to be steel.

—

Charles Stanley

MORE THOUGHTS ABOUT LOVE

Only joyous love redeems.

Catherine Marshall

To have fallen in love hints to our hearts that all of earthly life is not hopelessly fallen. Love is the laughter of God.

Beth Moore

Real love has staying power. Authentic love is tough love. It refuses to look for ways to run away. It always opts for working through.

Charles Swindoll

The world does not understand theology or dogma, but it does understand love and sympathy.

D. L. Moody

A WORD TO THE WISE

Parental love should be demonstrated with deeds, not just announced with words. You demonstrate your love by giving of yourself and your time. While you're with your child, be sure to watch carefully and listen with your ears, your eyes, and your heart. And remember: wise parents pay careful attention to the things their children don't say.

VERSE 21

Weeping may endure for a night,
but joy comes in the morning.

Psalm 30:5 NKJV

BEYOND GRIEF

Grief visits all of us who live long and love deeply. When we lose a loved one, or when we experience any other profound loss, darkness overwhelms us for a while, and it seems as if our purpose for living has vanished. Thankfully, God has other plans.

The Christian faith, as communicated through the words of the Holy Bible, is a healing faith. It offers comfort in times of trouble, courage for our fears, hope instead of hopelessness. For Christians, the grave is not a final resting-place, it is a place of transition. Through the healing words of God's promises, Christians understand that the Lord continues to manifest His plan in good times and bad.

God intends that you have a meaningful, abundant life, but He expects you to do your part in claiming those blessings. So, as you work through your grief, you will find it helpful to utilize all the resources that God has placed along your path. God makes help available, but it's up to you to find it and then to accept it.

First and foremost, you should lean upon the love, help, and support of family members, friends, fellow church members, and your pastor. Other resources include:

Various local counseling services including, but not limited to, pastoral counselors, psychologists, and community mental health facilities.

Group counseling programs which may deal with your specific loss.

Your personal physician.

The local bookstore or library (which will contain specific reading material about your grief and about your particular loss).

If you are experiencing the intense pain of a recent loss, or if you are still mourning a loss from long ago, perhaps you are now ready to begin the next stage of your journey with God. If so, be mindful of this fact: As a wounded survivor, you will have countless opportunities to serve others. And by serving others, you will bring purpose and meaning to the suffering you've endured.

More Thoughts About Overcoming Grief

God's Word never said we were not to grieve our losses. It says we are not to grieve as those who have no hope (1 Thessalonians 4:13). Big Difference.

Beth Moore

There is no way around suffering. We have to go through it to get to the other side.

Barbara Johnson

There is no pit so deep that God's love is not deeper still.

Corrie ten Boom

In times of deepest suffering it is the faithful carrying out of ordinary duties that brings the greatest consolation.

Elisabeth Elliot

You learn your theology most where your sorrows take you.

Martin Luther

A Word to the Wise

When you grieve, God remains steadfast . . . and He can comfort you.

VERSE 22

Jesus said to him, "'You shall love the Lord your God with all your heart, with all your soul, and with all your mind.' This is the first and great commandment."

Matthew 22:37-38 NKJV

LOVING GOD

Christ's words are unambiguous: "Love the Lord your God with all your heart and with all your soul and with all your mind." But sometimes, despite our best intentions, we fall short of God's plan for our lives when we become embittered with ourselves, with our neighbors, or most especially with our Creator.

If we are to please God, we must cleanse ourselves of the negative feelings that separate us from others and from Him. In 1 Corinthians 13, we are told that love is the foundation upon which all our relationships are to be built: our relationships with others and our relationship with our Maker.

So today and every day, fill your heart with love; never yield to bitterness; and praise the Son of God who, in His infinite wisdom, made love His greatest commandment.

Man was created by God
to know and love Him
in a permanent,
personal relationship.

—

Anne Graham Lotz

MORE THOUGHTS ABOUT LOVING GOD

When an honest soul can get still before the living Christ, we can still hear Him say simply and clearly, "Love the Lord your God with all your heart and with all your soul and with all your mind . . . and love one another as I have loved you."

Gloria Gaither

Loving Him means the thankful acceptance of all things that His love has appointed.

Elisabeth Elliot

Joy is a by-product not of happy circumstances, education or talent, but of a healthy relationship with God and a determination to love Him no matter what.

Barbara Johnson

I love Him because He first loved me, and He still does love me, and He will love me forever and ever.

Bill Bright

A WORD TO THE WISE

Because God first loved you, you should love Him. And one way that you demonstrate your love is by obeying Him.

VERSE 23

Be strong and courageous, and do the work.
Do not be afraid or discouraged,
for the Lord God, my God, is with you.

1 Chronicles 28:20 NIV

BEYOND THE FEAR OF FAILURE

As we consider the uncertainties of the future, we are confronted with a powerful temptation: the temptation to "play it safe." Unwilling to move mountains, we fret over molehills. Unwilling to entertain great hopes for the tomorrow, we focus on the unfairness of the today. Unwilling to trust God completely, we take timid half-steps when God intends that we make giant leaps.

Today, ask God for the courage to step beyond the boundaries of your doubts. Ask Him to guide you to a place where you can realize your full potential—a place where you are freed from the fear of failure. Ask Him to do His part, and promise Him that you will do your part. Don't ask Him to lead you to a "safe" place; ask Him to lead you to the "right" place . . . and remember: those two places are seldom the same.

Only a person who
dares to risk is free.

—

Joey Johnson

MORE THOUGHTS ABOUT FEAR OF FAILURE

There comes a time when we simply have to face the challenges in our lives and stop backing down.

John Eldredge

With each new experience of letting God be in control, we gain courage and reinforcement for daring to do it again and again.

Gloria Gaither

Risk must be taken because the greatest hazard in life is to risk nothing.

John Maxwell

Do not be one of those who, rather than risk failure, never attempt anything.

Thomas Merton

A WORD TO THE WISE

If you're too afraid of failure, you may not live up to your potential. Remember that failing isn't nearly as bad as failing to try.

VERSE 24

The LORD is gracious and full of compassion,
slow to anger and great in mercy.
The LORD is good to all,
and His tender mercies are over all His works.

Psalm 145:8-9 NKJV

GOD'S MERCY

In Psalm 145, we are taught that God is merciful. His hand offers forgiveness and salvation. God's mercy, like His love, is infinite and everlasting—it knows no boundaries.

Romans 3:23 reminds us of a universal truth: "All have sinned, and come short of the glory of God" (KJV). All of us, even the most righteous among us, are sinners. But despite our imperfections, our merciful Father in heaven offers us salvation through the person of His Son.

As Christians, we have been blessed by a merciful, loving God. Now, it's our turn to share His love and His mercy with a world that needs both. May we accept His gifts and share them with our friends, with our families, and with all the people He chooses to place along our paths.

MORE THOUGHTS ABOUT GOD'S MERCY

How happy we are when we realize that He is responsible, that He goes before, that goodness and mercy shall follow us!

Mrs. Charles E. Cowman

Is your child learning of the love of God through your love, tenderness, and mercy?

James Dobson

When terrible things happen, there are two choices, and only two: We can trust God, or we can defy Him. We believe that God is God, He's still got the whole world in His hands and knows exactly what He's doing, or we must believe that He is not God and that we are at the awful mercy of mere chance.

Elisabeth Elliot

Trust the past to the mercy of God, the present to his love, and the future to His Providence.

St. Augustine

Mercy is an attribute of God, an infinite and inexhaustible energy within the divine nature which disposes God to be actively compassionate.

A. W. Tozer

Angels descending, bring from above, Echoes of mercy, whispers of love.

Fanny Crosby

Looking back over my life, all I can see is mercy and grace written in large letters everywhere. May God help me have the same kind of heart toward those who wound or offend me.

Jim Cymbala

The Creator has given to us the awesome responsibility of representing him to our children. Our Heavenly Father is a God of unlimited love, and our children must become acquainted with His mercy and tenderness through our own love toward them.

James Dobson

Storm the throne of grace and persevere therein, and mercy will come down.

John Wesley

A WORD TO THE WISE

God forgives sin when you ask . . . so ask! God stands ready to forgive . . . the next move is yours.

VERSE 25

*Blessed is the man who walks not
in the counsel of the ungodly, nor stands in the path
of sinners, nor sits in the seat of the scornful;
but his delight is in the law of the Lord,
and in His law he meditates day and night.*

Psalm 1:1-2 NKJV

WALKING WITH THE RIGHTEOUS

Peer pressure can be a good thing or a bad thing, depending upon your peers. If your peers encourage you to make integrity a habit—and if they encourage you to follow God's will and to obey His commandments—then you'll experience positive peer pressure, and that's good. But, if you are involved with people who encourage you to do foolish things, you're facing a different kind of peer pressure . . . and you'd better beware. When you feel pressured to do things, or to say things, that lead you away from God, you're aiming straight for trouble.

Okay, Mom: here's a question for you: Are you satisfied to follow that crowd? If so, you may pay a heavy price unless you've picked the right crowd. And while you're deciding whom to follow, be sure you're determined to follow the One from Galilee, too. Jesus will guide your steps and bless your undertakings if you let Him. Your challenge, of course, is to let Him.

To sum it up, here's your choice: you can choose to please God first (and by doing so, strengthen your character), or you can fall prey to peer pressure. The choice is yours—and so are the consequences.

MORE THOUGHTS ABOUT PEER PRESSURE

It is comfortable to know that we are responsible to God and not to man. It is a small matter to be judged of man's judgement.

Lottie Moon

We, as God's people, are not only to stay far away from sin and sinners who would entice us, but we are to be so like our God that we mourn over sin.

Kay Arthur

You will get untold flak for prioritizing God's revealed and present will for your life over man's . . . but, boy, is it worth it.

Beth Moore

When we are set free from the bondage of pleasing others, when we are free from currying others' favor and others' approval—then no one will be able to make us miserable or dissatisfied. And then, if we know we have pleased God, contentment will be our consolation.

Kay Arthur

Do you want to be wise? Choose wise friends.

Charles Swindoll

For better or worse, you will eventually become more and more like the people you associate with. So why not associate with people who make you better, not worse?

Marie T. Freeman

You must never sacrifice your relationship with God for the sake of a relationship with another person.

Charles Stanley

A WORD TO THE WISE

Be a good example: If you are burdened with a "people-pleasing" personality, outgrow it. Realize that you can't please all of the people all of the time (including your children), nor should you attempt to.

VERSE 26

Even though I walk through
the valley of the shadow of death,
I will fear no evil, for you are with me;
your rod and your staff, they comfort me.

Psalm 23:4 NIV

TRUST THE SHEPHERD

In the 23rd Psalm, David teaches us that God is like a watchful shepherd caring for His flock. No wonder these verses have provided comfort and hope for generations of believers.

You are precious in the eyes of God. You are His priceless creation, made in His image, and protected by Him. God watches over every step you make and every breath you take, so you need never be afraid. But sometimes, fear has a way of slipping into the minds and hearts of even the most devout believers—and you are no exception.

As a busy mom, you know from firsthand experience that life is not always easy. But as a recipient of God's grace, you also know that you are protected by a loving Heavenly Father.

On occasion, you will confront circumstances that trouble you to the very core of your soul. When you are afraid, trust in God. When you are worried, turn your concerns over to Him. When you are anxious, be still and listen for the quiet assurance of God's promises. And then, place your life in His hands. He is your shepherd today and throughout eternity. Trust the Shepherd.

MORE THOUGHTS ABOUT GOD'S COMFORT

Put your hand into the hand of God. He gives the calmness and serenity of heart and soul.

Mrs. Charles E. Cowman

When I am criticized, injured, or afraid, there is a Father who is ready to comfort me.

Max Lucado

To know that God rules over all—that there are no accidents in life, that no tactic of Satan or man can ever thwart the will of God—brings divine comfort.

Kay Arthur

When God allows extraordinary trials for His people, He prepares extraordinary comforts for them.

Corrie ten Boom

We all go through pain and sorrow, but the presence of God, like a warm, comforting blanket, can shield us and protect us, and allow the deep inner joy to surface, even in the most devastating circumstances.

Barbara Johnson

You don't have to be alone in your hurt! Comfort is yours. Joy is an option. And it's all been made possible by your Savior. He went without comfort so you might have it. He postponed joy so you might share in it. He willingly chose isolation so you might never be alone in your hurt and sorrow.

Joni Eareckson Tada

Pour out your heart to God and tell Him how you feel. Be real, be honest, and when you get it all out, you'll start to feel the gradual covering of God's comforting presence.

Bill Hybels

A WORD TO THE WISE

God will always comfort you so that you, in turn, can have the strength to comfort others.

VERSE 27

But those who wait on the Lord
shall renew their strength;
they shall mount up with wings like eagles,
they shall run and not be weary,
they shall walk and not faint.

Isaiah 40:31 NKJV

STRENGTH FROM GOD

Even the most inspired Christian moms can, from time to time, find themselves running on empty. The demands of daily life can drain us of our strength and rob us of the joy that is rightfully ours in Christ. When we find ourselves tired, discouraged, or worse, there is a source from which we can draw the power needed to recharge our spiritual batteries. That source is God.

God intends that His children lead joyous lives filled with abundance and peace. But sometimes, abundance and peace seem very far away. It is then that we must turn to God for renewal, and when we do, He will restore us if we allow Him to do so.

Today, like every other day, is literally brimming with possibilities. Whether we realize it or not, God is always working in us and through us; our job is to let Him do His work without undue interference. Yet we are imperfect beings who, because of our limited vision, often resist God's will. And oftentimes, because of our stubborn insistence on squeezing too many activities into a 24-hour day, we allow ourselves to become exhausted or frustrated, or both.

Are you tired or troubled? Turn your heart toward God in prayer. Are you weak or worried? Take the time—or, more accurately, make the time—to delve deeply into God's Holy Word. Are you spiritually depleted? Call upon fellow believers to support you, and call upon Christ to renew your spirit and your life. Are you simply overwhelmed by the demands of the day? Pray for the wisdom to simplify your life. Are you exhausted? Pray for the wisdom to rest a little more and worry a little less.

When you do these things, you'll discover that the Creator of the universe stands always ready and always able to create a new sense of wonderment and joy in you.

Worry does not empty tomorrow of its sorrow;
it empties today of its strength.

Corrie ten Boom

MORE THOUGHTS ABOUT STRENGTH

No matter how heavy the burden, daily strength is given, so I expect we need not give ourselves any concern as to what the outcome will be. We must simply go forward.

Annie Armstrong

When we spend time with Christ, He supplies us with strength and encourages us in the pursuit of His ways.

Elizabeth George

God conquers only what we yield to Him. Yet, when He does, and when our surrender is complete, He fills us with a new strength that we could never have known by ourselves. His conquest is our victory!

Shirley Dobson

The same God who empowered Samson, Gideon, and Paul seeks to empower my life and your life, because God hasn't changed.

Bill Hybels

A WORD TO THE WISE

When you are tired, fearful, or discouraged, God can restore your strength.

VERSE 28

Be still, and know that I am God . . . .

Psalm 46:10 KJV

BE STILL

We live in a noisy world, a world filled with distractions, frustrations, complications, and obligations. But we must not allow our clamorous world to separate us from God's peace. Instead, we must "be still" so that we might sense the presence of God.

If we are to maintain righteous minds and compassionate hearts, we must take time each day for prayer and for meditation. We must make ourselves still in the presence of our Creator. We must quiet our minds and our hearts so that we might sense God's love, God's will, and God's Son.

Has the busy pace of life robbed you of the peace that might otherwise be yours through Jesus Christ? If so, it's time to reorder your priorities. Nothing is more important than the time you spend with your Savior. So be still, Mom, and claim the inner peace that is your spiritual birthright: the peace of Jesus Christ. It is offered freely; it has been paid for in full; it is yours for the asking. So ask. And then share.

When frustrations develop into
problems that stress you out,
the best way to cope is to stop,
catch your breath,
and do something for yourself,
not out of selfishness,
but out of wisdom.

—

Barbara Johnson

MORE THOUGHTS ABOUT QUIET TIME

The manifold rewards of a serious, consistent prayer life demonstrate clearly that time with our Lord should be our first priority.

Shirley Dobson

I don't see how any Christian can survive, let alone live life as more than a conqueror, apart from a quiet time alone with God.

Kay Arthur

The Lord Jesus, available to people much of the time, left them, sometimes a great while before day, to go up to the hills where He could commune in solitude with His Father.

Elisabeth Elliot

Since the quiet hour spent with God is the preacher's power-house, the devil centers his attention on that source of strength.

Vance Havner

A WORD TO THE WISE

Be still and listen to God. He has something important to say to you.

VERSE 29

And now abide faith, hope, love, these three;
but the greatest of these is love.

1 Corinthians 13:13 NKJV

THE GREATEST OF THESE IS LOVE

The familiar words of 1st Corinthians 13 remind us of the importance of love. Faith is important, of course. So, too, is hope. But love is more important still.

Christ showed His love for us on the cross, and, as Christians, we are called upon to return Christ's love by sharing it. We are commanded (not advised, not encouraged . . . commanded!) to love one another just as Christ loved us (John 13:34). That's a tall order, but as Christians, we are obligated to follow it.

Sometimes love is easy (puppies and sleeping children come to mind), and sometimes love is hard (fallible human beings come to mind). But God's Word is clear: We are to love all our friends and neighbors, not just the lovable ones. So today, take time to spread Christ's message by word and by example. And the greatest of these is, of course, is example.

Love is the seed of all hope.
It is the enticement to trust,
to risk, to try, and to go on.

—

Gloria Gaither

MORE THOUGHTS ABOUT LOVE

Those who abandon ship the first time it enters a storm miss the calm beyond. And the rougher the storms weathered together, the deeper and stronger real love grows.

Ruth Bell Graham

Love is an attribute of God. To love others is evidence of a genuine faith.

Kay Arthur

Live your lives in love, the same sort of love which Christ gives us, and which He perfectly expressed when He gave Himself as a sacrifice to God.

Corrie ten Boom

He who is filled with love is filled with God Himself.

St. Augustine

A WORD TO THE WISE

Be imaginative. There are so many ways to say, "I love you." Find them. Put love notes in lunch pails and on pillows; hug relentlessly; laugh, play, and pray with abandon. Remember that love is highly contagious, and that your task, as a parent, is to ensure that your children catch it.

*But seek first the kingdom of God
and His righteousness,
and all these things shall be added to you.
Therefore do not worry about tomorrow,
for tomorrow will worry about its own things.
Sufficient for the day is its own trouble.*

Matthew 6:33-34 NKJV

BEYOND WORRY

Because we are imperfect human beings struggling with imperfect circumstances, we worry. Even though we, as Christians, have the assurance of salvation—even though we, as Christians, have the promise of God's love and protection—we find ourselves fretting over the inevitable frustrations of everyday life. Jesus understood our concerns when He spoke the reassuring words found in the 6th chapter of Matthew.

Where is the best place to take your worries? Take them to God. Take your troubles to Him; take your fears to Him; take your doubts to Him; take your weaknesses to Him; take your sorrows to Him . . . and leave them all there. Seek protection from the One who offers you eternal salvation; build your spiritual house upon the Rock that cannot be moved.

Perhaps you are concerned about your future, your health, or your finances. Or perhaps you are simply a "worrier" by nature. If so, make Matthew 6 a regular part of your daily Bible reading. This beautiful passage will remind you that God still sits in His heaven and you are His beloved child. Then, perhaps, you will worry a little less and trust God a little more, and that's as it should be because God is trustworthy . . . and you are protected.

MORE THOUGHTS ABOUT WORRY

This life of faith, then, consists in just this—being a child in the Father's house. Let the ways of childish confidence and freedom from care, which so please you and win your heart when you observe your own little ones, teach you what you should be in your attitude toward God.

Hannah Whitall Smith

Today is mine. Tomorrow is none of my business. If I peer anxiously into the fog of the future, I will strain my spiritual eyes so that I will not see clearly what is required of me now.

Elisabeth Elliott

The beginning of anxiety is the end of faith, and the beginning of true faith is the end of anxiety.

George Mueller

Never yield to gloomy anticipation. Place your hope and confidence in God. He has no record of failure.

Mrs. Charles E. Cowman

We are not called to be burden-bearers, but cross-bearers and light-bearers. We must cast our burdens on the Lord.

Corrie ten Boom

God is bigger than your problems. Whatever worries press upon you today, put them in God's hands and leave them there.

Billy Graham

Worry is the senseless process of cluttering up tomorrow's opportunities with leftover problems from today.

Barbara Johnson

A WORD TO THE WISE

Work hard, pray harder, and if you have any worries, take them to God—and leave them there.

VERSE 31

*Trust in the Lord with all your heart,
and lean not on your own understanding;
In all your ways acknowledge Him,
and He shall direct your paths.*

Proverbs 3:5-6 NKJV

TRUST HIM

It's easy to talk about trusting God, but when it comes to actually trusting Him, that's considerably harder. Why? Because genuine trust in God requires more than words; it requires a willingness to follow God's lead and a willingness to obey His commandments. (These, by the way, are not easy things to do.)

Have you spent more time talking about Christ than walking in His footsteps? If so, God wants to have a little chat with you. And, if you're unwilling to talk to Him, He may take other actions in order to grab your attention.

Thankfully, whenever you're willing to talk with God, He's willing to listen. And, the instant that you decide to place Him squarely in the center of your life, He will respond to that decision with blessings that are too unexpected to predict and too numerous to count.

The next time you find your courage tested to the limit, lean upon God's promises. Trust His Son. Remember that God is always near and that He is your protector and your deliverer. When you are worried, anxious, or afraid, call upon Him. God can handle your troubles infinitely better than you can, so turn them over to Him. Remember that God rules both mountaintops and valleys—with limitless wisdom and love—now and forever.

MORE THOUGHTS ABOUT TRUSTING GOD

Sometimes the very essence of faith is trusting God in the midst of things He knows good and well we cannot comprehend.

Beth Moore

A prayerful heart and an obedient heart will learn, very slowly and not without sorrow, to stake everything on God Himself.

Elisabeth Elliot

Are you serious about wanting God's guidance to become the person he wants you to be? The first step is to tell God that you know you can't manage your own life; that you need his help.

Catherine Marshall

Do not be afraid, then, that if you trust, or tell others to trust, the matter will end there. Trust is only the beginning and the continual foundation. When we trust Him, the Lord works, and His work is the important part of the whole matter.

Hannah Whitall Smith

Brother, is your faith looking upward today? / Trust in the promise of the Savior. / Sister, is the light shining bright on your way? / Trust in the promise of thy Lord.

Fanny Crosby

God is God. He knows what he is doing. When you can't trace his hand, trust his heart.

Max Lucado

Beware of trusting in yourself, and see that you trust in the Lord.

Oswald Chambers

A WORD TO THE WISE

Because God is trustworthy—and because He has made promises to you that He intends to keep—you are protected.

VERSE 32

I am the vine, you are the branches.
He who abides in Me, and I in him,
bears much fruit;
for without Me you can do nothing.
John 15:5 NKJV

HE IS THE VINE

He was the Son of God, but He wore a crown of thorns. He was the Savior of mankind, yet He was put to death on a roughhewn cross. He offered His healing touch to an unsaved world, and yet the same hands that had healed the sick and raised the dead were pierced with nails.

Jesus Christ, the Son of God, was born into humble circumstances. He walked this earth, not as a ruler of men, but as the Savior of mankind. His crucifixion, a torturous punishment that was intended to end His life and His reign, instead became the pivotal event in the history of all humanity. Christ sacrificed His life on the cross so that we might have eternal life. This gift, freely given by God's only begotten Son, is the priceless possession of everyone who accepts Him as Lord and Savior.

Why did Christ endure the humiliation and torture of the cross? He did it for you. His love is as near as your next breath, as personal as your next thought, more essential than your next heartbeat. And what must you do in response to the Savior's gifts? You must accept His love, praise His name, and share His message of salvation. And, you must conduct yourself in a manner that demonstrates to all the world that your acquaintance with the Master is not a passing fancy but that it is, instead, the cornerstone and the touchstone of your life.

More Thoughts About Jesus

Jesus makes God visible. But that truth does not make Him somehow less than God. He is equally supreme with God.

Anne Graham Lotz

Tell me the story of Jesus. Write on my heart every word. Tell me the story most precious, sweetest that ever was heard.

Fanny Crosby

The crucial question for each of us is this: What do you think of Jesus, and do you yet have a personal acquaintance with Him?

Hannah Whitall Smith

Had Jesus been the Word become word, He would have spun theories about life, but since he was the Word become flesh, he put shoes on all his theories and made them walk.

E. Stanley Jones

Christians see sin for what it is: willful rebellion against the rulership of God in their lives. And in turning from their sin, they have embraced God's only means of dealing with sin: Jesus.

Kay Arthur

In your greatest weakness, turn to your greatest strength, Jesus, and hear Him say, "My grace is sufficient for you, for My strength is made perfect in weakness" (2 Corinthians 12:9, NKJV).

Lisa Whelchel

Jesus was the perfect reflection of God's nature in every situation He encountered during His time here on earth.

Bill Hybels

A WORD TO THE WISE

Jesus is the light of the world. As a caring parent, it's up to you to make certain that He's the light of your family, too.

Ask, and it will be given to you;
seek, and you will find;
knock, and it will be opened to you.
For everyone who asks receives,
and he who seeks finds,
and to him who knocks it will be opened.

Matthew 7:7-8 NKJV

ASK HIM FOR
THE THINGS YOU NEED

How often do you ask God for His help and His wisdom? Occasionally? Intermittently? Whenever you experience a crisis? Hopefully not. Hopefully, you've acquired the habit of asking for God's assistance early and often. And hopefully, you have learned to seek His guidance in every aspect of your life.

In Matthew 7, God promises that He will guide you if you let Him. Your job is to let Him. But sometimes, you will be tempted to do otherwise. Sometimes, you'll be tempted to go along with the crowd; other times, you'll be tempted to do things your way, not God's way. When you feel those temptations, resist them.

God has promised that when you ask for His help, He will not withhold it. So ask. Ask Him to meet the needs of your day. Ask Him to lead you, to protect you, and to correct you. And trust the answers He gives.

God stands at the door and waits. When you knock, He opens. When you ask, He answers. Your task, of course, is to seek His guidance prayerfully, confidently, and often.

MORE THOUGHTS ABOUT ASKING GOD

By asking in Jesus' name, we're making a request not only in His authority, but also for His interests and His benefit.

Shirley Dobson

When will we realize that we're not troubling God with our questions and concerns? His heart is open to hear us— his touch nearer than our next thought—as if no one in the world existed but us. Our very personal God wants to hear from us personally.

Gigi Graham Tchividjian

All we have to do is to acknowledge our need, move from self-sufficiency to dependence, and ask God to become our hiding place.

Bill Hybels

God uses our most stumbling, faltering faith-steps as the open door to His doing for us "more than we ask or think."

Catherine Marshall

Often I have made a request of God with earnest pleadings even backed up with Scripture, only to have Him say "No" because He had something better in store.

Ruth Bell Graham

God makes prayer as easy as possible for us. He's completely approachable and available, and He'll never mock or upbraid us for bringing our needs before Him.

Shirley Dobson

Some people think God does not like to be troubled with our constant asking. But, the way to trouble God is not to come at all.

D. L. Moody

A WORD TO THE WISE

If you sincerely want to guard your steps, ask for God's help.

VERSE 34

You shall have no other gods before Me.
Exodus 20:3 NKJV

PUTTING GOD FIRST

As you fulfill the responsibilities of caring for your family, what is your top priority? Do you and your loved ones strive to place God first in every aspect of your lives, or do you usually focus on other priorities? The answer to this simple question will determine the quality and the direction of your own life and the lives of your family members.

As you contemplate your family's relationship with God, remember this: all of mankind is engaged in the practice of worship. Some families choose to worship God and, as a result, they reap the joy that He intends for His children. Other families distance themselves from God by worshipping such things as earthly possessions or personal gratification. . . . and when they do so, they suffer.

In the book of Exodus, God warns that we should place no gods before Him. Yet all too often, we place our Lord in second, third, or fourth place as we worship the gods of pride, possessions, prestige, or power.

When we place our desires for material possessions above our love for the Father—or when we yield to the inevitable temptations and complications of life here in the New Millennium—we find ourselves engaged in a struggle that is similar to the one Jesus faced when He was tempted by Satan. In the wilderness, Satan offered Jesus earthly power and unimaginable riches, but Jesus turned Satan away and chose instead to worship God. We must do likewise by putting God first and by worshipping only Him.

Does God rule over your heart and your home? Make certain that the honest answer to this question is a resounding yes. In the collective life of every Christian family, God should come first—and it's up to you to make certain that He comes first at your house.

A man's spiritual health is exactly proportional to his love for God.

C. S. Lewis

MORE THOUGHTS ABOUT PUTTING GOD FIRST

Make God's will the focus of your life day by day. If you seek to please Him and Him alone, you'll find yourself satisfied with life.

Kay Arthur

It is impossible to please God doing things motivated by and produced by the flesh.

Bill Bright

Jesus Christ is the first and last, author and finisher, beginning and end, alpha and omega, and by Him all other things hold together. He must be first or nothing. God never comes next!

Vance Havner

You must never sacrifice your relationship with God for the sake of a relationship with another person.

Charles Stanley

A WORD TO THE WISE

As you establish priorities for your day and your life, God deserves first place. And you deserve the experience of putting Him there.

VERSE 35

*I am come that they might have life,
and that they might have it more abundantly.*

John 10:10 KJV

ACCEPTING
GOD'S ABUNDANCE

God sent His Son so that mankind might enjoy the abundant life that Jesus describes in the familiar words of John 10:10. But, God's gifts are not guaranteed; His gifts must be claimed by those who choose to follow Christ.

Do you sincerely seek the riches that our Savior offers to those who give themselves to Him? Then follow Him completely and obey Him without reservation. When you do, you will receive the love and the abundance that He has promised. Seek first the salvation that is available through a personal, passionate relationship with Christ, and then claim the joy, the peace, and the spiritual abundance that the Shepherd offers His sheep.

Today, Mom, as you organize your day and care for your family, accept God's promise of spiritual abundance . . . you may be certain that when you do your part, God will do His part.

God's riches are beyond
anything we could ask
or even dare to imagine!
If my life gets gooey and stale,
I have no excuse.

—

Barbara Johnson

MORE THOUGHTS ABOUT ABUNDANCE

The gift of God is eternal life, spiritual life, abundant life through faith in Jesus Christ, the Living Word of God.

Anne Graham Lotz

It would be wrong to have a "poverty complex," for to think ourselves paupers is to deny either the King's riches or to deny our being His children.

Catherine Marshall

Jesus intended for us to be overwhelmed by the blessings of regular days. He said it was the reason he had come: "I am come that they might have life, and that they might have it more abundantly."

Gloria Gaither

A WORD TO THE WISE

When Jesus talked about abundance, was He talking about "money"? The answer is no. When Christ talked about abundance, He was concerned with people's spiritual well-being, not their financial well-being. That's a lesson that you must learn . . . and it's a lesson that you must share with your child.

VERSE 36

Choose for yourselves today
the one you will worship . . . .
As for me and my family,
we will worship the Lord.

Joshua 24:15 Holman CSB

A FAMILY THAT SERVES GOD

In a world filled with countless obligations and frequent frustrations, we may be tempted to take our families for granted. But God intends otherwise.

Our families are precious gifts from our Father in heaven. If we are to be the righteous men and women that God intends, we must care for our loved ones by making time for them, even when the demands of the day are great.

Undeniably, these are difficult days for Christian households: never have distractions and temptations been greater. But, thankfully, God is bigger than all our challenges.

No family is perfect, Mom, and neither is yours. But, despite the inevitable challenges, obligations, and hurt feelings of family life, your clan is God's blessing to you. That little band of men, women, kids, and babies is a priceless treasure on temporary loan from the Father above. Give thanks to the Giver for the gift of family . . . and act accordingly.

MORE THOUGHTS ABOUT FAMILY

A home is a place where we find direction.

Gigi Graham Tchividjian

One way or the other, God, who thought up the family in the first place, has the very best idea of how to bring sense to the chaos of broken relationships we see all around us. I really believe that if I remain still and listen a lot, He will share some solutions with me so I can share them with others.

Jill Briscoe

More than any other single factor in a person's formative years, family life forges character.

John Maxwell

Every Christian family ought to be, as it were, a little church, consecrated to Christ, and wholly influenced and governed by His rules.

Jonathan Edwards

Calm and peaceful, the home should be the one place where people are certain they will be welcomed, received, protected, and loved.

Ed Young

Living life with a consistent spiritual walk deeply influences those we love most.

Vonette Bright

Live in the present and make the most of your opportunities to enjoy your family and friends.

Barbara Johnson

The family that prays together, stays together.

Anonymous

A family is a place where principles are hammered and honed on the anvil of everyday living.

Charles Swindoll

A WORD TO THE WISE

Your family is a precious gift from above, a gift that should be treasured, nurtured, and loved.

*For by grace you are saved through faith,
and this is not from yourselves; it is God's gift—
not from works, so that no one can boast.*

Ephesians 2:8-9 Holman CSB

THE GIFT OF GRACE

In the second chapter of Ephesians, God promises that we will be saved by faith, not by works. It's no wonder, then, that someone once said that GRACE stands for God's Redemption At Christ's Expense. It's true—God sent His Son so that we might be redeemed from our sins. In doing so, our Heavenly Father demonstrated His infinite mercy and His infinite love. We have received countless gifts from God, but none can compare with the gift of salvation. God's grace is the ultimate gift, and we owe Him the ultimate in thanksgiving.

The gift of eternal life is the priceless possession of everyone who accepts God's Son as Lord and Savior. We return our Savior's love by welcoming Him into our hearts and sharing His message and His love. When we do so, we are blessed not only today, but forever.

MORE THOUGHTS ABOUT GRACE

The Christian life is motivated, not by a list of do's and don'ts, but by the gracious outpouring of God's love and blessing.

Anne Graham Lotz

In the depths of our sin, Christ died for us. He did not wait for persons to get as close as possible through obedience to the law and righteous living.

Beth Moore

Just as I am, without one plea, but that Thy blood was shed for me. And that Thou bid'st me come to Thee, O Lamb of God, I come! I come!

Charlotte Elliott

God's grand strategy, birthed in his grace toward us in Christ, and nurtured through the obedience of disciplined faith, is to release us into the redeemed life of our heart, knowing it will lead us back to him even as the North Star guides a ship across the vast unknown surface of the ocean.

John Eldredge

Grace is but glory begun, and glory is but grace perfected.

Jonathan Edwards

The cross was heavy, the blood was real, and the price was extravagant. It would have bankrupted you or me, so he paid it for us. Call it simple. Call it a gift. But don't call it easy. Call it what it is. Call it grace.

Max Lucado

God shields us from most of the things we fear, but when He chooses not to shield us, He unfailingly allots grace in the measure needed.

Elisabeth Elliot

How beautiful it is to learn that grace isn't fragile, and that in the family of God we can fail and not be a failure.

Gloria Gaither

No one is beyond his grace. No situation, anywhere on earth, is too hard for God.

Jim Cymbala

A WORD TO THE WISE

Remember that His grace is enough . . . God promises that His grace is sufficient for your needs. Believe Him.

*Everyone must be quick to hear,
slow to speak, and slow to anger, for man's anger
does not accomplish God's righteousness.*

James 1:19-20 Holman CSB

THE FUTILITY OF ANGER

Motherhood is vastly rewarding, but every mother knows that it can be, at times, frustrating. No family is perfect, and even the most loving mother's patience can, on occasion, wear thin.

Your temper is either your master or your servant. Either you control it, or it controls you. And the extent to which you allow anger to rule your life will determine, to a surprising degree, the quality of your relationships with others and your relationship with God.

If you've allowed anger to become a regular visitor at your house, you should pray for wisdom, for patience, and for a heart that is so filled with forgiveness that it contains no room for bitterness. God will help you terminate your tantrums if you ask Him to—and that's a good thing because anger and peace cannot coexist in the same mind.

So the next time you're tempted to lose your temper over the minor inconveniences of life, don't. Turn away from anger, hatred, bitterness, and regret. Turn instead to God. He's waiting with open arms . . . patiently.

MORE THOUGHTS ABOUT ANGER

Anger unresolved will only bring you woe.

Kay Arthur

Life is too short to spend it being angry, bored, or dull.

Barbara Johnson

When you get hot under the collar, make sure your heart is prayer-conditioned.

Anonymous

When something robs you of your peace of mind, ask yourself if it is worth the energy you are expending on it. If not, then put it out of your mind in an act of discipline. Every time the thought of "it" returns, refuse it.

Kay Arthur

When you strike out in anger, you may miss the other person, but you will always hit yourself.

Jim Gallery

Get rid of the poison of built-up anger and the acid of long-term resentment.

Charles Swindoll

Anger's the anaesthetic of the mind.

C. S. Lewis

The hard part about being a praying wife is maintaining a pure heart. If you have resentment, anger, unforgiveness, or an ungodly attitude—even if there's good reason for it—you'll have a difficult time seeing answers to your prayers. But if you can release those feelings to God in total honesty, there is nothing that can change a marriage more dramatically.

Stormie Omartian

Anger is the noise of the soul; the unseen irritant of the heart; the relentless invader of silence.

Max Lucado

A WORD TO THE WISE

If you can control your anger, you'll help your children see the wisdom in controlling theirs.

*Therefore, whatever you want others
to do for you, do also the same for them—
this is the Law and the Prophets.*

Matthew 7:12 Holman CSB

THE GOLDEN RULE

The words of Matthew 7:12 remind us that, as believers in Christ, we are commanded to treat others as we wish to be treated. This commandment is, indeed, the Golden Rule for Christians of every generation. When we weave the thread of kindness into the very fabric of our lives, we give glory to the One who gave His life for ours.

Is the Golden Rule one of the rules that governs your household? Hopefully so. Obeying the Golden Rule is a proven way to improve all your relationships, including your relationships with the people who happen to live inside the four walls of your home. But the reverse is also true: if you or your loved ones ignore the Golden Rule, you're headed for trouble, and fast.

God's Word makes it clear: we are to treat our loved ones with respect, kindness, fairness, and courtesy. And

He knows we can do so if we try. So if you're wondering how you should treat your loved ones—or anybody else, for that matter—just ask the person you see every time you look into the mirror. The answer you receive will tell you exactly what to do.

It is one of the most beautiful compensations
of life that no one can sincerely try to help
another without helping herself.

Barbara Johnson

MORE THOUGHTS ABOUT THE GOLDEN RULE

The Golden Rule starts at home, but it should never stop there.

Marie T. Freeman

Your light is the truth of the Gospel message itself as well as your witness as to who Jesus is and what He has done for you. Don't hide it.

Anne Graham Lotz

In your desire to share the gospel, you may be the only Jesus someone else will ever meet. Be real and be involved with people.

Barbara Johnson

The golden rule to follow to obtain spiritual understanding is not one of intellectual pursuit, but one of obedience.

Oswald Chambers

A WORD TO THE WISE

The Golden Rule . . . is as good as gold—in fact, it's better than gold. And as a responsible parent, you should make certain that your child knows that the Golden Rule is, indeed, golden.

VERSE 40

Cast thy burden upon the LORD,
and he shall sustain thee:
he shall never suffer the righteous to be moved.

Psalm 55:22 KJV

WHERE TO PLACE
YOUR BURDENS

God's Word contains promises upon which we, as Christians, can and must depend. The Bible is a priceless gift, a tool that God intends for us to use in every aspect of our lives. Too many Christians, however, keep their spiritual tool kits tightly closed and out of sight.

Psalm 55:22 instructs us to cast our burdens upon the Lord. And that's perfect advice for men, women, and children alike.

Are you tired? Discouraged? Fearful? Be comforted and trust the promises that God has made to you. Are you worried or anxious? Be confident in God's power. He will never desert you. Do you see a difficult future ahead? Be courageous and call upon God. He will protect you and then use you according to His purposes. Are you confused?

Listen to the quiet voice of your Heavenly Father. He is not a God of confusion. Talk with Him; listen to Him; trust Him, and trust His promises. He is steadfast, and He is your Protector . . . forever.

MORE THOUGHTS ABOUT GOD'S SUPPORT

God uses our most stumbling, faltering faith-steps as the open door to His doing for us "more than we ask or think."

Catherine Marshall

Measure the size of the obstacles against the size of God.

Beth Moore

God wants to reveal Himself as your heavenly Father. When you are hurting, you can run to Him and crawl up into His lap. When you wonder which way to turn, you can grasp His strong hand, and He'll guide you along life's path. When everything around you is falling apart, you'll feel your Father's arm around your shoulder to hold you together.

Lisa Whelchel

Without God, life has no purpose, and without purpose, life has no meaning.

Rick Warren

The last and greatest lesson that the soul has to learn is the fact that God, and God alone, is enough for all its needs. This is the lesson that all His dealings with us are meant to teach; and this is the crowning discovery of our whole Christian life. God is enough!

Hannah Whitall Smith

When God speaks to you through the Bible, prayer, circumstances, the church, or in some other way, he has a purpose in mind for your life.

Henry Blackaby and Claude King

Once we recognize our need for Jesus, then the building of our faith begins. It is a daily, moment-by-moment life of absolute dependence upon Him for everything.

Catherine Marshall

Faith is not merely you holding on to God—it is God holding on to you.

E. Stanley Jones

A WORD TO THE WISE

God can handle it. Corrie ten Boom advised, "God's all-sufficiency is a major. Your inability is a minor. Major in majors, not in minors." Enough said.

VERSE 41

You will show me the path of life;
in Your presence is fullness of joy;
at Your right hand are pleasures forevermore.
Psalm 16:11 NKJV

HE WILL SHOW YOU
THE PATH

L ife is best lived on purpose, not by accident: the
sooner we discover what God intends for us to do
with our lives, the better. But God's purposes aren't
always clear to us. Sometimes, the responsibilities of caring
for our loved ones leave us precious little time to discern
God's will for ourselves. At other times, we may struggle
mightily against God in a vain effort to find success and
happiness through our own means, not His.

Whenever we struggle against God's plans, we suffer.
When we resist God's calling, our efforts bear little fruit.
Our best strategy, therefore, is to seek God's wisdom and
follow Him wherever He chooses to lead. When we do so,
we are blessed.

As a loving mother, you know intuitively that God
has important plans for you and your family. But how

can you know precisely what God's intentions are? The answer, of course, is that even the most well-intentioned believers face periods of uncertainty about the direction of their lives. So, too, will you.

When you arrive at one of life's inevitable crossroads, that is precisely the moment when you should turn your thoughts and prayers toward God. When you do, He will make Himself known to you in a time and manner of His choosing. And when you discover God's purpose for your life, you will experience abundance, peace, joy, and power—God's power. And that's the only kind of power that really matters.

MORE THOUGHTS ABOUT LIVING ON PURPOSE

Yesterday is just experience but tomorrow is glistening with purpose—and today is the channel leading from one to the other.

Barbara Johnson

Only God's chosen task for you will ultimately satisfy. Do not wait until it is too late to realize the privilege of serving Him in His chosen position for you.

Beth Moore

His life is our light—our purpose and meaning and reason for living.

Anne Graham Lotz

In the very place where God has put us, whatever its limitations, whatever kind of work it may be, we may indeed serve the Lord Christ.

Elisabeth Elliot

How much of our lives are, well, so daily. How often our hours are filled with the mundane, seemingly unimportant things that have to be done, whether at home or work. These very "daily" tasks could become a celebration of praise. "It is through consecration," someone has said, "that drudgery is made divine."

Gigi Graham Tchividjian

Continually restate to yourself what the purpose of your life is.

Oswald Chambers

A WORD TO THE WISE

God has a plan for your life, a definite purpose that you can fulfill . . . or not. Your challenge is to pray for God's guidance and to follow wherever He leads.

VERSE 42

*Now by this we know that we know Him,
if we keep His commandments.*

1 John 2:3 NKJV

OBEYING GOD

At one time or another, we all face a similar temptation—the temptation to follow some of God's rules and disregard others. But if we're wise, we won't pick and choose among the Bible's commandments . . . we'll do our best to obey them all, not just the ones that are easy or convenient. When we do, we are most certainly blessed by our loving, heavenly Father.

Today, Mom, take every step of your journey with God as your traveling companion. Read His Word and take it seriously. Support only those activities that further your own spiritual growth. Be a positive example to your children, to your friends, to your neighbors, and to your community. Then, prepare yourself for the countless blessings God has promised to all those who trust—and obey—Him completely.

You may not always see
immediate results,
but all God wants is your
obedience and faithfulness.

—

Vonette Bright

MORE THOUGHTS ABOUT OBEDIENCE

The cross that Jesus commands you and me to carry is the cross of submissive obedience to the will of God, even when His will includes suffering and hardship and things we don't want to do.

Anne Graham Lotz

I don't always like His decisions, but when I choose to obey Him, the act of obedience still "counts" with Him even if I'm not thrilled about it.

Beth Moore

Jesus is Victor. Calvary is the place of victory. Obedience is the pathway of victory. Bible study and prayer is the preparation for victory.

Corrie ten Boom

A WORD TO THE WISE

Your children will learn about life from many sources; the most important source should be you. But remember that the lectures you give are never as important as the ones you live.

All Scripture is given by inspiration of God,
and is profitable for doctrine, for reproof,
for correction, for instruction in righteousness,
that the man of God may be complete,
thoroughly equipped for every good work.

2 Timothy 3:16-17 NKJV

THE USE OF SCRIPTURE

God's wisdom is found in a book like no other: the Holy Bible. The Bible is a roadmap for life here on earth and for life eternal. As Christians, we are called upon to study God's Holy Word, to trust His Word, to follow its commandments, and to share its Good News with the world and with our families.

The words of Matthew 4:4 remind us that, "Man shall not live by bread alone but by every word that proceedeth out of the mouth of God." (KJV). And, as Christian parents, we must study the Bible and meditate upon its meaning for our lives. Otherwise, we deprive ourselves and our children of a priceless gift from our Creator.

So, as you continue to search for tools to improve your parenting skills, remember that you already own a copy of the world's greatest parenting guidebook, a complete and perfect epistle from the Creator. When you study your Bible every day, you'll continue to derive fresh insights about your family and your life. By establishing the habit of daily Bible study, you'll transform yourself into a better spouse, a better parent, and a better Christian.

Warren Wiersbe observed, "When the child of God looks into the Word of God, he sees the Son of God. And, he is transformed by the Spirit of God to share in the glory of God." God's Holy Word is, indeed, a transforming, life-changing, one-of-a-kind treasure. And, a passing acquaintance with the Good Book is insufficient for Christians who seek to obey God's Word and to understand His will. After all, neither man nor parents should live by bread alone . . .

Either God's Word keeps you from sin,
or sin keeps you from God's Word.

Corrie ten Boom

MORE THOUGHTS ABOUT GOD'S WORD

The Holy Spirit is the Spirit of Truth, which means He always works according to and through the Word of God whether you feel Him or not.

Anne Graham Lotz

God's Word is a light not only to our path but also to our thinking. Place it in your heart today, and you will never walk in darkness.

Joni Eareckson Tada

Help me, Lord, to be a student of Your Word, that I might be a better servant in Your world.

Jim Gallery

Walking in faith brings you to the Word of God. There you will be healed, cleansed, fed, nurtured, equipped, and matured.

Kay Arthur

A WORD TO THE WISE

God intends for you to use His Word as your guidebook for life . . . your intentions should be the same.

VERSE 44

To everything there is a season,
a time for every purpose under heaven.
Ecclesiastes 3:1 NKJV

TRUST GOD'S TIMING

If you sincerely seek to be a woman of faith, then you must learn to trust God's timing. You will be sorely tempted, however, to do otherwise. Because you are an imperfect human being, you are impatient for things to happen. But, God knows better.

God has created a world that unfolds according to His own timetable, not ours . . . thank goodness! We mortals might make a terrible mess of things. God does not.

God's plan does not always happen in the way that you would like or at the time of your own choosing. Your task—as a caring mom who trusts in a benevolent, all-knowing Father—is to wait patiently for God to reveal Himself. And reveal Himself He will. Always. But until God's perfect plan is made known, you must walk in faith and never lose hope. And you must continue to trust Him. Always.

MORE THOUGHTS ABOUT GOD'S TIMING

When our plans are interrupted, his are not. His plans are proceeding exactly as scheduled, moving us always— including those minutes or hours or years which seem most useless or wasted or unendurable—toward the goal of true maturity.

Elisabeth Elliot

Your times are in His hands. He's in charge of the timetable, so wait patiently.

Kay Arthur

God's delays and His ways can be confusing because the process God uses to accomplish His will can go against human logic and common sense.

Anne Graham Lotz

When we read of the great Biblical leaders, we see that it was not uncommon for God to ask them to wait, not just a day or two, but for years, until God was ready for them to act.

Gloria Gaither

The stops of a good man are ordered by the Lord as well as his steps.

George Mueller

Grass that is here today and gone tomorrow does not require much time to mature. A big oak tree that lasts for generations requires much more time to grow and mature. God is concerned about your life through eternity. Allow Him to take all the time He needs to shape you for His purposes. Larger assignments will require longer periods of preparation.

Henry Blackaby

God does not promise to keep us out of the storms and floods, but He does promise to sustain us in the storm, and then bring us out in due time for His glory when the storm has done its work.

Warren Wiersbe

He wants us to have a faith that does not complain while waiting, but rejoices because we know our times are in His hands—nail-scarred hands that labor for our highest good.

Kay Arthur

A WORD TO THE WISE

You don't know precisely what you need—or when you need it—but God does. So trust His timing.

VERSE 45

Guard your heart above all else,
for it is the source of life.

Proverbs 4:23 Holman CSB

GUARD YOUR HEART

You are near and dear to God. He loves you more than you can imagine, and He wants the very best for you. And one more thing, Mom: God wants you to guard your heart—but the world may tempt you to let down your guard.

The world has a way of capturing your attention and distorting your thoughts. Society wants you and your loved ones to focus on worldly matters. God, on the other hand, wants you to focus on Him.

Your task, of course, is to make sure that you focus your thoughts and energies on God's priorities, things that enrich your life and enhance your faith. So today, Mom, be watchful and obedient. Guard your heart by giving it to your Heavenly Father; it is safe with Him.

To lose heart
is to lose everything.

—

John Eldredge

More Thoughts About
Guarding Your Heart

Our actions are seen by people, but our motives are monitored by God.

Franklin Graham

A man's poverty before God is judged by the disposition of his heart, not by his coffers.

St. Augustine

The God who dwells in heaven is willing to dwell also in the heart of the humble believer.

Warren Wiersbe

We can't stop the Adversary from whispering in our ears, but we can refuse to listen, and we can definitely refuse to respond.

Liz Curtis Higgs

A Word to the Wise

Today, think about the value of living a life that is pleasing to God. And while you're at it, think about the rewards that are likely to be yours when you do the right thing day in and day out.

VERSE 46

Then He said to them all,
"If anyone desires to come after Me,
let him deny himself, and take up his cross daily,
and follow Me. For whoever desires to
save his life will lose it, but whoever loses his life
for My sake will save it."
Luke 9:23-24 NKJV

FOLLOW HIM

J esus walks with you. Are you walking with Him? Hopefully, you will choose to walk with Him today and every day of your life.

Jesus loved you so much that He endured unspeakable humiliation and suffering for you. How will you respond to Christ's sacrifice? Will you follow the instructions of Luke 9:23 by taking up His cross and following Him? Or will you choose another path? When you place your hopes squarely at the foot of the cross, when you place Jesus squarely at the center of your life, you will be blessed. If you seek to be a worthy disciple of Jesus, you must acknowledge that He never comes "next." He is always first.

Do you hope to fulfill God's purpose for your life? Do you seek a life of abundance and peace? Do you intend to be Christian, not just in name, but in deed? Then follow Christ. Follow Him by picking up His cross today and every day that you live. When you do, you will quickly discover that Christ's love has the power to change everything, including you.

MORE THOUGHTS ABOUT FOLLOWING JESUS

As we live moment by moment under the control of the Spirit, His character, which is the character of Jesus, becomes evident to those around us.

Anne Graham Lotz

A disciple is a follower of Christ. That means you take on His priorities as your own. His agenda becomes your agenda. His mission becomes your mission.

Charles Stanley

Peter said, "No, Lord!" But he had to learn that one cannot say "No" while saying "Lord" and that one cannot say "Lord" while saying "No."

Corrie ten Boom

Think of this—we may live together with Him here and now, a daily walking with Him who loved us and gave Himself for us.

Elisabeth Elliot

Will you, with a glad and eager surrender, hand yourself and all that concerns you over into his hands? If you will do this, your soul will begin to know something of the joy of union with Christ.

Hannah Whitall Smith

The Christian faith is meant to be lived moment by moment. It isn't some broad, general outline—it's a long walk with a real Person. Details count: passing thoughts, small sacrifices, a few encouraging words, little acts of kindness, brief victories over nagging sins.

Joni Eareckson Tada

We have in Jesus Christ a perfect example of how to put God's truth into practice.

Bill Bright

A WORD TO THE WISE

Do you want your children to follow in the footsteps of Jesus? Then you must lead the way. Actions speak louder than sermons . . . much louder.

VERSE 47

God is our refuge and strength,
a very present help in trouble.

Psalm 46:1 NKJV

GOD IS OUR REFUGE

The words of Psalm 46:1 promise that God is our refuge, a refuge that we all need. From time to time, all of us face adversity, discouragement, or disappointment. And throughout life, we all must endure life-changing personal losses that leave us breathless. When we do, God stands ready to protect us. Psalm 147 assures us that, "He heals the brokenhearted, and binds their wounds" (v. 3, NIV).

Are you anxious? Take those anxieties to God. Are you troubled? Take your troubles to Him. Does the world seem to be trembling beneath your feet? Seek protection from the One who cannot be moved.

The same God who created the universe stands ready and willing to comfort you and to restore your strength. During life's most difficult days, your Heavenly Father remains steadfast. And, in His own time and according to His master plan, He will heal you if you invite Him into your heart.

Measure the size of the obstacles
against the size of God.

—

Beth Moore

MORE THOUGHTS ABOUT TOUGH TIMES

Faith is a strong power, mastering any difficulty in the strength of the Lord who made heaven and earth.

Corrie ten Boom

If all struggles and sufferings were eliminated, the spirit would no more reach maturity than would the child.

Elisabeth Elliot

God will never let you sink under your circumstances. He always provides a safety net and His love always encircles.

Barbara Johnson

Even in the winter, even in the midst of the storm, the sun is still there. Somewhere, up above the clouds, it still shines and warms and pulls at the life buried deep inside the brown branches and frozen earth. The sun is there! Spring will come.

Gloria Gaither

A WORD TO THE WISE

When you experience tough times (and you will), a positive attitude makes a big difference in the way you tackle your problems.

VERSE 48

No one can be a slave of two masters,
since either he will hate one and love the other,
or be devoted to one and despise the other.
You cannot be slaves of God and of money.

Matthew 6:24 Holman CSB

KEEPING MONEY IN PERSPECTIVE

Your money can be used as a blessing to yourself and to your loved ones, but beware: You live in a society that places far too much importance on money and the things that money can buy. God does not. God cares about people, not possessions, and so must you.

Money, in and of itself, is not evil, but worshipping money most certainly is. So today, as you prioritize matters of importance for you and yours, remember that God is almighty, but the dollar is not.

When we worship God, we are blessed. But if we worship "the almighty dollar," we inevitably pay a price for our misplaced priorities—and our punishment inevitably comes sooner rather than later. Our challenge, then, is to keep money in proper perspective which, by the way, is God's perspective.

Your priorities, passions, goals,
and fears are shown clearly
in the flow of your money.

—

Dave Ramsey

MORE THOUGHTS ABOUT KEEPING MONEY IN PERSPECTIVE

Have you prayed about your resources lately? Find out how God wants you to use your time and your money. No matter what it costs, forsake all that is not of God.

Kay Arthur

TITHE! Anyone can honk!

Anonymous

Attitude is always God's concern. Christ's statement dealing with the rich young ruler was based on that man's attitude, his motivation, and the purpose behind his money.

Larry Burkett

If a person gets his attitude toward money straight, it will help straighten out almost every other area of his life.

Billy Graham

A WORD TO THE WISE

The Bible clearly warns us never to fall in love with money.

VERSE 49

Love is patient; love is kind.
Love does not envy; is not boastful;
is not conceited; does not act improperly;
is not selfish; is not provoked; does not keep
a record of wrongs; finds no joy in unrighteousness,
but rejoices in the truth; bears all things,
believes all things, hopes all things,
endures all things.

1 Corinthians 13:4-7 Holman CSB

LOVE IS . . .

Love is a choice. Either you choose to behave lovingly toward others . . . or not; either you behave yourself in ways that enhance your relationships . . . or not. But make no mistake: genuine love requires effort. Simply put, if you wish to build lasting relationships, you must be willing to do your part.

Since the days of Adam and Eve, God has allowed His children to make choices for themselves, and so it is with you. As you interact with family and friends, you have choices to make . . . lots of them. If you choose wisely, you'll be rewarded; if you choose unwisely, you'll bear the consequences.

God does not intend for you to experience mediocre relationships; He created you for far greater things. Building lasting relationships requires compassion, wisdom, empathy, kindness, courtesy, and forgiveness (lots of forgiveness). If that sounds a lot like work, it is—which is perfectly fine with God. Why? Because He knows that you are capable of doing that work, and because He knows that the fruits of your labors will enrich the lives of your loved ones and the lives of generations yet unborn.

Love is a steady wish
for the loved person's ultimate good.

C. S. Lewis

MORE THOUGHTS ABOUT LOVE

How do you spell love? When you reach the point where the happiness, security, and development of another person is as much of a driving force to you as your own happiness, security, and development, then you have a mature love. True love is spelled G-I-V-E. It is not based on what you can get, but rooted in what you can give to the other person.

Josh McDowell

The truth of the Gospel is intended to free us to love God and others with our whole heart.

John Eldredge

Truth becomes hard if it is not softened by love, and love becomes soft if not strengthened by truth.

E. Stanley Jones

A WORD TO THE WISE

Of course it's good to tell your kids how you feel about them, but that's not enough. You should also show your children how you feel with your good deeds and your kind words.

VERSE 50

If you have faith as a mustard seed,
you will say to this mountain,
"Move from here to there," and it will move;
and nothing will be impossible for you.
Matthew 17:20 NKJV

MOUNTAIN-MOVING FAITH

Because we live in a demanding world, all of us have mountains to climb and mountains to move. Moving those mountains requires faith.

Are you a mountain mover whose faith is evident for all to see? Or, are you a spiritual shrinking violet? God needs more men and women who are willing to move mountains for His glory and for His kingdom.

Jesus taught His disciples that if they had faith, they could move mountains. You can too. When you place your faith, your trust, indeed your life in the hands of Christ Jesus, you'll be amazed at the marvelous things He can do. So strengthen your faith through praise, through worship, through Bible study, and through prayer. And trust God's plans. With Him, all things are possible, and He stands ready to open a world of possibilities to you . . . if you have faith.

Concentration camp survivor Corrie ten Boom relied on faith during her long months of imprisonment and torture. Later, despite the fact that four of her family members had died in Nazi death camps, Corrie's faith was unshaken. She wrote, "There is no pit so deep that God's love is not deeper still." Christians take note: Genuine faith in God means faith in all circumstances, happy or sad, joyful or tragic.

If your faith is being tested to the point of breaking, remember that your Savior is near. If you reach out to Him in faith, He will give you peace and strength. Reach out today. If you touch even the smallest fragment of the Master's garment, He will make you whole. And then, with no further ado, let the mountain moving begin.

MORE THOUGHTS ABOUT FAITH

There are a lot of things in life that are difficult to understand. Faith allows the soul to go beyond what the eyes can see.

John Maxwell

Just as our faith strengthens our prayer life, so do our prayers deepen our faith. Let us pray often, starting today, for a deeper, more powerful faith.

Shirley Dobson

Faith is seeing light with the eyes of your heart, when the eyes of your body see only darkness.

Barbara Johnson

Grace calls you to get up, throw off your blanket of helplessness, and to move on through life in faith.

Kay Arthur

If God chooses to remain silent, faith is content.

Ruth Bell Graham

Faith does not concern itself with the entire journey. One step is enough.

Mrs. Charles E. Cowman

The popular idea of faith is of a certain obstinate optimism: the hope, tenaciously held in the face of trouble, that the universe is fundamentally friendly and things may get better.

J. I. Packer

A WORD TO THE WISE

If your faith is strong enough, you and God—working together—can move mountains.

VERSE 51

Heaven and earth will pass away,
but My words will never pass away.

Matthew 24:35 Holman CSB

TRUST GOD'S WORD

A re you a woman who trusts God's Word without reservation? Hopefully so, because the Bible is unlike any other book—it is a guidebook for life here on earth and for life eternal.

As a Christian, you are instructed to study God's Holy Word, to trust His Word, to follow its commandments, and to share its Good News with the world. The Psalmist writes, "Your word is a lamp to my feet and a light to my path" (Psalm 119:105 NASB). Is the Bible your lamp? If not, you are depriving yourself of a priceless gift from the Creator.

Vance Havner observed, "It takes calm, thoughtful, prayerful meditation on the Word to extract its deepest nourishment." How true. God's Word can be a roadmap to a place of righteousness and abundance. Make it your roadmap. God's wisdom can be a light to guide your steps. Claim it as your light today, tomorrow, and every day of your life—and then walk confidently in the footsteps of God's only begotten Son.

MORE THOUGHTS ABOUT GOD'S WORD

For whatever life holds for you and your family in the coming days, weave the unfailing fabric of God's Word through your heart and mind. It will hold strong, even if the rest of life unravels.

Gigi Graham Tchividjian

Words fail to express my love for this holy Book, my gratitude for its author, for His love and goodness. How shall I thank him for it?

Lottie Moon

God can see clearly no matter how dark or foggy the night is. Trust His Word to guide you safely home.

Lisa Whelchel

I believe the reason so many are failing today is that they have not disciplined themselves to read God's Word consistently, day in and day out, and to apply it to every situation in life.

Kay Arthur

The Bible became a living book and a guide for my life.

Vonette Bright

The promises of Scripture are not mere pious hopes or sanctified guesses. They are more than sentimental words to be printed on decorated cards for Sunday School children. They are eternal verities. They are true. There is no perhaps about them.

Peter Marshall

It takes calm, thoughtful, prayerful meditation on the Word to extract its deepest nourishment.

Vance Havner

God has given us all sorts of counsel and direction in his written Word; thank God, we have it written down in black and white.

John Eldredge

A WORD TO THE WISE

On your bookshelf you have God's roadmap for life here on earth and for life eternal. How you choose to use your Bible is, of course, up to you . . . and so are the consequences.

Go, therefore, and make disciples of all nations,
baptizing them in the name of the Father
and of the Son and of the Holy Spirit,
teaching them to observe everything I have
commanded you. And remember,
I am with you always, to the end of the age.

Matthew 28:19-20 Holman CSB

THE GREAT COMMISSION

Are you a bashful Christian, one who is afraid to speak up for your Savior? Do you leave it up to others to share their testimonies while you stand on the sidelines, reluctant to share yours? Too many of us are slow to obey the last commandment of the risen Christ; we don't do our best to "make disciples of all the nations."

Christ's Great Commission applies to Christians of every generation, including our own. As believers, we are commanded to share the Good News with our families, with our neighbors, and with the world. Jesus invited His disciples to become fishers of men. We, too, must accept the Savior's invitation, and we must do so today. Tomorrow may indeed be too late.

You cannot keep silent
once you have experienced
salvation of Jesus Christ.

—

Warren Wiersbe

MORE THOUGHTS ABOUT
THE GREAT COMMISSION

Our commission is quite specific. We are told to be His witness to all nations. For us, as His disciples, to refuse any part of this commission frustrates the love of Jesus Christ, the Son of God.

Catherine Marshall

There are many timid souls whom we jostle morning and evening as we pass them by; but if only the kind word were spoken they might become fully persuaded.

Fanny Crosby

Your light is the truth of the Gospel message itself as well as your witness as to who Jesus is and what He has done for you. Don't hide it.

Anne Graham Lotz

There is nothing anybody else can do that can stop God from using us. We can turn everything into a testimony.

Corrie ten Boom

A WORD TO THE WISE

The best day to respond to Christ's Great Commission is this day.

VERSE 53

Therefore, whether you eat or drink,
or whatever you do, do all to the glory of God.

1 Corinthians 10:31 NKJV

HIS PRIORITIES
AND YOUR HEALTH

When it comes to matters of physical, spiritual, and emotional health, Christians possess an infallible guidebook: the Holy Bible. And, when it comes to matters concerning fitness—whether physical, emotional, or spiritual fitness—God's Word can help us establish clear priorities that can guide our steps and our lives.

It's easy to talk about establishing clear priorities for maintaining physical and spiritual health, but it's much more difficult to live according to those priorities. For busy believers living in a demanding world, placing first things first can be difficult indeed. Why? Because so many people are expecting so many things from us!

If you're having trouble prioritizing your day—or if you're having trouble sticking to a plan that enhances your spiritual and physical health—perhaps you've been trying to organize your life according to your own plans, not God's. A better strategy, of course, is to take your daily obligations and place them in the hands of the One who created you. To do so, you must prioritize your day according to God's commandments, and you must seek His will and His wisdom in all matters.

Would you like to embark upon a personal journey to better fitness? If so, you should remind yourself that on every step of that journey, you have a traveling companion: your Heavenly Father. Turn the concerns of this day over to Him—prayerfully, earnestly, and often. And trust Him to give you the strength you need to become the kind of person He wants you to become.

MORE THOUGHTS ABOUT HEALTH

Our primary motivation should not be for more energy or to avoid a heart attack but to please God with our bodies.

Carole Lewis

You can't buy good health at the doctor's office—you've got to earn it for yourself.

Marie T. Freeman

The key to healthy eating is moderation and managing what you eat every day.

John Maxwell

If you want to form a new habit, get to work. If you want to break a bad habit, get on your knees.

Marie T. Freeman

God wants you to give Him your body. Some people do foolish things with their bodies. God wants your body as a holy sacrifice.

Warren Wiersbe

People are funny. When they are young, they will spend their health to get wealth. Later, they will gladly pay all they have trying to get their health back.

John Maxwell

Ultimate healing and the glorification of the body are certainly among the blessings of Calvary for the believing Christian. Immediate healing is not guaranteed.

Warren Wiersbe

A WORD TO THE WISE

God has given you a body, and He's placed you in charge of caring for it. Your body is a temple that should be treated with respect.

VERSE 54

Man does not see what the Lord sees,
for man sees what is visible,
but the Lord sees the heart.

1 Samuel 16:7 Holman CSB

KEEPING UP APPEARANCES

The words of 1 Samuel 16:7 remind us God sees the heart. We human beings, on the other hand, are often far more concerned with outward appearances.

Are you worried about keeping up appearances? And as a result, do you spend too much time, energy, or money on things that are intended to make you look good? If so, you are certainly not alone. Ours is a society that focuses intently upon appearances. We are told time and again that we can't be "too thin or too rich." But in truth, the important things in life have little to do with food, fashion, fame, or fortune.

Today, spend less time trying to please the world and more time trying to please your earthly family and your Father in heaven. Focus on pleasing your God and your loved ones, and don't worry too much about trying to impress the folks you happen to pass on the street. It takes too much energy—and too much life—to keep up appearances. So don't waste your energy or your life.

The single most important element
in any human relationship is honesty—
with oneself, with God, and with others.

Catherine Marshall

MORE THOUGHTS ABOUT APPEARANCES

Outside appearances, things like the clothes you wear or the car you drive, are important to other people but totally unimportant to God. Trust God.

Marie T. Freeman

Our ultimate aim in life is not to be healthy, wealthy, prosperous, or problem free. Our ultimate aim in life is to bring glory to God.

Anne Graham Lotz

Once you loosen up, let yourself be who you are: the wonderful, witty woman whom God will use to encourage and uplift other people.

Barbara Johnson

Being loved by Him whose opinion matters most gives us the security to risk loving, too—even loving ourselves.

Gloria Gaither

A WORD TO THE WISE

How you appear to other people doesn't make much difference, but how you appear to God makes all the difference.

VERSE 55

Whoever conceals an offense promotes love,
but whoever gossips about it separates friends.

Proverbs 17:9 Holman CSB

ABOVE AND BEYOND GOSSIP

The Bible clearly tells us that gossip is wrong. But when it comes to the special confidences that you share with your very closest friends, gossip can be disastrous.

The Bible reminds us that "Reckless words pierce like a sword, but the tongue of the wise brings healing" (Proverbs 12:18 NIV). Therefore, if we are to solve more problems than we start, we must measure our words carefully, and we must never betray a confidence. But sometimes even the most thoughtful among us may speak first and think second (with decidedly mixed results).

When we speak too quickly, we may say things that that would be better left unsaid. When we forgo the wonderful opportunity to consider our thoughts before we give voice to them, we're putting ourselves and our relationships in danger.

A far better strategy, of course, is to do the more difficult thing: to think first and to speak next. When we do so, we give ourselves ample time to compose our thoughts and to consult our Creator before we say something that we might soon regret.

MORE THOUGHTS ABOUT GOSSIP

The things that we feel most deeply we ought to learn to be silent about, at least until we have talked them over thoroughly with God.

Elisabeth Elliot

It is time that the followers of Jesus revise their language and learn to speak respectfully of non-Christian peoples.

Lottie Moon

When you talk, choose the very same words that you would use if Jesus were looking over your shoulder. Because He is.

Marie T. Freeman

I still believe we ought to talk about Jesus. The old country doctor of my boyhood days always began his examination by saying, "Let me see your tongue." That's a good way to check a Christian: the tongue test. Let's hear what he is talking about.

Vance Havner

Change the heart, and you change the speech.

Warren Wiersbe

The great test of a man's character is his tongue.

Oswald Chambers

A little kindly advice is better than a great deal of scolding.

Fanny Crosby

Like dynamite, God's power is only latent power until it is released. You can release God's dynamite power into people's lives and the world through faith, your words, and prayer.

Bill Bright

If you can't think of something nice to say, keep thinking.

Criswell Freeman

A WORD TO THE WISE

Make your home a gossip-free zone. Gossip is a learned behavior. Make sure that your kids don't learn it from you!

VERSE 56

The sensible see danger and take cover;
the foolish keep going and are punished.

Proverbs 27:12 Holman CSB

PLAN AHEAD . . .
AND WORK HARD

Are you willing to plan for the future—and are you willing to work diligently to accomplish the plans that you've made? The Book of Proverbs teaches that the plans of hardworking people (like you) are rewarded.

If you desire to reap a bountiful harvest from life, you must plan for the future while entrusting the final outcome to God. Then, you must do your part to make the future better (by working dutifully), while acknowledging the sovereignty of God's hands over all affairs, including your own.

Are you in a hurry for success to arrive at your doorstep? Don't be. Instead, work carefully, plan thoughtfully, and wait patiently. Remember that you're not the only one working on your behalf: God, too, is at work. And with Him as your partner, your ultimate success is guaranteed.

You can't start building
a better tomorrow
if you wait till tomorrow
to start building.

—

Marie T. Freeman

MORE THOUGHTS ABOUT PLANNING

The only way you can experience abundant life is to surrender your plans to Him.

Charles Stanley

Allow your dreams a place in your prayers and plans. God-given dreams can help you move into the future He is preparing for you.

Barbara Johnson

Plan ahead—it wasn't raining when Noah built the ark.

Anonymous

God has a plan for your life . . . do you?

Criswell Freeman

Our problem is that we become too easily enamored with our own plans.

Henry Blackaby

A WORD TO THE WISE

It isn't that complicated: If you plan your steps carefully, and if you follow your plan conscientiously, you will probably succeed. If you don't, you probably won't.

177

I have set before you life and death,
blessing and curse. Choose life so that
you and your descendants may live,
love the Lord your God, obey Him,
and remain faithful to Him. For He is your life,
and He will prolong your life in the land
the Lord swore to give to your fathers
Abraham, Isaac, and Jacob.

Deuteronomy 30:19-20 Holman CSB

MAKING GOOD CHOICES

Life is a series of choices. From the instant we wake in the morning until the moment we nod off to sleep at night, we make countless decisions: decisions about the things we do, decisions about the words we speak, and decisions about the thoughts we choose to think. Simply put, the quality of those decisions determines the quality of our lives.

As believers who have been saved by a loving and merciful God, we have every reason to make wise choices. Yet sometimes, amid the inevitable hustle and bustle of life here on earth, we allow ourselves to behave in ways that we know are displeasing to God. When we do, we forfeit—albeit temporarily—the joy and the peace that we might otherwise experience through Him.

As you consider the next step in your life's journey, take time to consider how many things in this life you can control: your thoughts, your words, your priorities, and your actions, for starters. And then, if you sincerely want to discover God's purpose for your life, make choices that are pleasing to Him. He deserves no less . . . and neither, Mom, do you.

Every day of our lives
we make choices about
how we're going to live that day.
Luci Swindoll

MORE THOUGHTS ABOUT CHOICES

Commitment to His lordship on Easter, at revivals, or even every Sunday is not enough. We must choose this day—and every day—whom we will serve. This deliberate act of the will is the inevitable choice between habitual fellowship and habitual failure.

Beth Moore

There may be no trumpet sound or loud applause when we make a right decision, just a calm sense of resolution and peace.

Gloria Gaither

No matter how many books you read, no matter how many schools you attend, you're never really wise until you start making wise choices.

Marie T. Freeman

God expresses His love in giving us the freedom to choose.

Charles Stanley

A WORD TO THE WISE

Every day you make hundreds of choices . . . and the quality of those choices determines the quality of your day and your life.

VERSE 58

Be sober! Be on the alert!
Your adversary the Devil is prowling around
like a roaring lion,
looking for anyone he can devour.

1 Peter 5:8 Holman CSB

BE ALERT FOR
THE ADVERSARY

Sometimes sin has a way of sneaking up on us. In the beginning, we don't intend to rebel against God—in fact, we don't think much about God at all. We think, instead, about the allure of sin, and we think (quite incorrectly) that sin is "harmless."

If we deny our sins, we allow those sins to flourish. And if we allow sinful behaviors to become habits, we invite certain hardships into our own lives and into the lives of our loved ones.

Sin tears down character. When we yield to the distractions and temptations of this troubled world, we suffer. But God has other intentions, and His plans for our lives do not include sin or denial.

As creatures of free will, we may disobey God whenever we choose, but when we do so, we put ourselves and our loved ones in peril. Why? Because disobedience invites disaster. We cannot sin against God without consequence. We cannot live outside His will without injury. We cannot distance ourselves from God without hardening our hearts. We cannot yield to the ever-tempting distractions of our world and, at the same time, enjoy God's peace.

Sometimes, in a futile attempt to justify our behaviors, we make a distinction between "big" sins and "little" ones. To do so is a mistake of "big" proportions. Sins of all shapes and sizes have the power to do us great harm. And in a world where sin is big business, that's certainly a sobering thought.

More Thoughts About Sin

Could it be that the greatest sin is simply not to love the Lord your God with all your heart, mind, soul, and strength?

Anne Graham Lotz

When it comes to sin, commit to not commit!

Anonymous

We cannot out-sin God's ability to forgive us.

Beth Moore

Sin is any deed or memory that hampers or binds human personality.

Catherine Marshall

Repentance is a complete surrender of my sinfulness to the only One who can cleanse me from all sin, and that is Jesus Christ.

Elisabeth Elliot

An exalted view of God brings a clear view of sin and a realistic view of self.

Henry Blackaby

There is nothing wrong with asking God's direction. But it is wrong to go our own way, then expect Him to bail us out.

Larry Burkett

A WORD TO THE WISE

Every day of your life, you will be tempted to rebel against God's teachings. Your job, simply put, is to guard your heart against the darkness as you focus on the light.

VERSE 59

Rejoice always, pray without ceasing,
in everything give thanks;
for this is the will of God in Christ Jesus for you.

1 Thessalonians 5:16-18 NKJV

PRAY OFTEN

Is prayer an integral part of your daily life, or is it a hit-or-miss habit? Do you "pray without ceasing," or is your prayer life an afterthought? Do you regularly pray in the quiet moments of the early morning, or do you bow your head only when others are watching?

As Christians, we are instructed to pray often. But it is important to note that genuine prayer requires much more than bending our knees and closing our eyes. Heartfelt prayer is an attitude of the heart.

If your prayers have become more a matter of habit than a matter of passion, you're robbing yourself of a deeper relationship with God. And how can you rectify this situation? By praying more frequently and more fervently. When you do, God will shower you with His blessings, His grace, and His love.

The quality of your spiritual life will be in direct proportion to the quality of your prayer life: the more you pray, the closer you will feel to God. So today, instead of turning things over in your mind, turn them over to God in prayer. Instead of worrying about your next decision, ask God to lead the way. Don't limit your prayers to the dinner table or the bedside table. Pray constantly about things great and small. God is always listening; it's up to you to do the rest.

God says we don't need to be
anxious about anything;
we just need to pray about everything.

Stormie Omartian

MORE THOUGHTS ABOUT PRAYER

What God gives in answer to our prayers will always be the thing we most urgently need, and it will always be sufficient.

Elisabeth Elliot

When the Holy Spirit comes to dwell within us, I believe we gain a built-in inclination to take our concerns and needs to the Lord in prayer.

Shirley Dobson

The center of power is not to be found in summit meetings or in peace conferences. It is not in Peking or Washington or the United Nations, but rather where a child of God prays in the power of the Spirit for God's will to be done in her life, in her home, and in the world around her.

Ruth Bell Graham

It is well said that neglected prayer is the birth-place of all evil.

C. H. Spurgeon

A WORD TO THE WISE

Absolutely no parental duty is more important than praying for your child.

VERSE 60

But the fruit of the Spirit is love,
joy, peace, patience, kindness,
goodness, faith, gentleness, self-control.
Against such things there is no law.

Galatians 5:22-23 Holman CSB

THE FRUITS OF THE SPIRIT

In Galatians 5, we are also told that when people live by the Spirit, they will bear "fruit of the Spirit." But what, exactly, is the fruit of the Spirit? It's a way of behaving yourself, a way of treating other people, a way of showing the world what it means to be a Christian. The Bible says, "The fruit of the Spirit is love, joy, peace, patience, kindness, goodness, faith, gentleness, self-control."

Today and every day, will you strive to be patient, joyful, loving, and kind? Will you really try to control yourself? And while you're at it, will you be peaceful, gentle, patient, and faithful? If so, you'll demonstrate to the world that the fruits of the Spirit can make a wonderful difference in the lives of good Christian people—people like you!

The Holy Spirit cannot be
located as a guest in a house.
He invades everything.

—

Oswald Chambers

MORE THOUGHTS ABOUT THE FRUITS OF THE SPIRIT

Some people have received Christ but have never reached spiritual maturity. We should grow as Christians every day, and we are not completely mature until we live in the presence of Christ.

Billy Graham

Though we, as Christians, are like Christ, having the first fruits of the Spirit, we are unlike Him, having the remainders of the flesh.

Thomas Watson

The more we abide in Christ, the more fruit we bear.

Warren Wiersbe

A WORD TO THE WISE

As an adult, you know that the journey toward spiritual maturity lasts a lifetime. And as a concerned parent, it's up to you to make sure that your child understands that the fruit of the spirit results in a dynamic growing relationship with God.

VERSE 61

Train up a child in the way he should go,
and when he is old he will not depart from it.

Proverbs 22:6 NKJV

TRAINING OUR CHILDREN

I n the 22nd chapter of Proverbs, we are instructed to train our children while they are still young. So, as responsible adults, we want to share God's wisdom with the next generation. But we cannot impart what we don't possess. So it's never enough to talk about God's rules; we must also be willing to live by them. Then, when our words match our deeds, we can teach our children using both proclamations and (more importantly) demonstrations.

When are the best times to teach your youngster? Deuteronomy 6:7 instructs you to teach God's wisdom, "When you sit in your house and when you walk along the road, when you lie down and when you get up" (Holman CSB). In other words, you should be ready to share God's teachings at any time: during regular family gathers (mealtimes, weekends, holidays, etc.) as well as those unplanned "teachable" moments that seem to pop up from time to time.

Deuteronomy 6:7 also makes it clear that you should teach your child when he lies down (with bedtime stories and prayers) and when he gets up (with morning family devotionals).

At what age should you begin teaching your child? As soon as possible! In fact, many experts believe that a significant portion of a person's character is formed by the tender age of six—so when it comes to teaching, the early years are golden. So, while God's grace can transform a person at any age, wise parents begin teaching their youngsters from the cradle onward.

What lessons can you teach a very young child? The simplest and most profound elements of God's moral order. These lessons include, but are not limited to such topics as kindness, truthfulness, God's love, the gift of eternal life, and, of course, the New Testament message of Jesus Christ.

Our faithfulness, or lack of it,
will have an overwhelming impact
on the heritage of our children.

Beth Moore

MORE THOUGHTS ABOUT CHILDREN

The balance of affirmation and discipline, freedom and restraint, encouragement and warning is different for each child and season and generation, yet the absolutes of God's Word are necessary and trustworthy at all times.

Gloria Gaither

The only real qualifications that parents need is a sincere and diligent desire to follow God's ways. God knew your strengths and weaknesses when you signed up to be a parent, and He still hired you.

Lisa Whelchel

Children are not casual guests in our home. They have been loaned to us temporarily for the purpose of loving them and instilling a foundation of values on which their future lives will be built.

James Dobson

A WORD TO THE WISE

It's hard work being a responsible parent, but the rewards always outweigh the costs. Simply put, your youngster is a marvelous gift from God. And, your opportunity to be a parent is yet another gift, for which you should give thanks.

VERSE 62

When I was a child, I spoke as a child,
I understood as a child, I thought as a child;
but when I became a man,
I put away childish things.

1 Corinthians 13:11 NKJV

STILL GROWING UP

The journey toward spiritual maturity lasts a lifetime. As Christians, we can and should continue to grow in the love and the knowledge of our Savior as long as we live. Norman Vincent Peale had the following advice for believers of all ages: "Ask the God who made you to keep remaking you." That advice, of course, is perfectly sound, but often ignored.

When we cease to grow, either emotionally or spiritually, we do ourselves a profound disservice. But, if we study God's Word, if we obey His commandments, and if we live in the center of His will, we will not be "stagnant" believers; we will, instead, be growing Christians . . . and that's exactly what God intends for us to be.

Life is a series of choices and decisions. Each day, we make countless decisions that can bring us closer to God . . . or not. When we live according to the principles contained in God's Holy Word, we embark upon a journey of spiritual maturity that results in life abundant and life eternal.

MORE THOUGHTS ABOUT MATURITY

The disappointment has come, not because God desires to hurt you or make you miserable or to demoralize you, or ruin your life, or keep you from ever knowing happiness. He wants you to be perfect and complete in every aspect, lacking nothing. It's not the easy times that make you more like Jesus, but the hard times.

Kay Arthur

We cannot hope to reach Christian maturity in any way other than by yielding ourselves utterly and willingly to His mighty working.

Hannah Whitall Smith

As God perfects us, He keeps us protected from the pride that might otherwise develop by veiling, to some extent, our progress in our own eyes. The light of the glory of His presence shines two ways: it sheds light on the knowledge of God so that we can learn to see Him more clearly, but it also sheds light on ourselves so that we can see our own sin more clearly.

Beth Moore

When I was young I was sure of everything; in a few years, having been mistaken a thousand times, I was not half so sure of most things as I was before; at present, I am hardly sure of anything but what God has revealed to me.

John Wesley

No matter what we are going through, no matter how long the waiting for answers, of one thing we may be sure. God is faithful. He keeps His promises. What He starts, He finishes . . . including His perfect work in us.

Gloria Gaither

Integrity and maturity are two character traits vital to the heart of a leader.

Charles Stanley

Growth in depth and strength and consistency and fruitfulness and ultimately in Christlikeness is only possible when the winds of life are contrary to personal comfort.

Anne Graham Lotz

A WORD TO THE WISE

If you want your youngster to become a mature Christian, then you should realize that your youngster is learning about spiritual maturity from a very important role model: you.

VERSE 63

Shepherd God's flock among you,
not overseeing out of compulsion but freely,
according to God's will;
not for the money but eagerly.

1 Peter 5:2 Holman CSB

CHRIST-CENTERED
LEADERSHIP

The old saying is familiar and true: imitation is the sincerest form of flattery. As believers, we are called to imitate, as best we can, the carpenter from Galilee. The task of imitating Christ is often difficult and sometimes impossible, but as Christians, we must continue to try.

Our world needs leaders who willingly honor Christ with their words and their deeds, but not necessarily in that order. If you seek to be such a leader, then you must begin by making yourself a worthy example to your family, to your friends, to your church, and to your community. After all, your words of instruction will never ring true unless you yourself are willing to follow them.

Christ-centered leadership is an exercise in service: service to God in heaven and service to His children here on earth. Christ willingly became a servant to His followers, and you must seek to do the same for yours.

Are you the kind of servant-leader whom you would want to follow? If so, congratulations: you are honoring your Savior by imitating Him. And that, of course, is the sincerest form of flattery.

You can never separate
a leader's actions from his character.

John Maxwell

MORE THOUGHTS ABOUT LEADERSHIP

A man ought to live so that everybody knows he is a Christian, and most of all, his family ought to know.

D. L. Moody

A wise leader chooses a variety of gifted individuals. He complements his strengths.

Charles Stanley

What do we Christians chiefly value in our leaders? The answer seems to be not their holiness, but their gifts and skills and resources. The thought that only holy people are likely to be spiritually useful does not loom large in our minds.

J. I. Packer

A true and safe leader is likely to be one who has no desire to lead, but is forced into a position of leadership by inward pressure of the Holy Spirit and the press of external situation.

A. W. Tozer

A WORD TO THE WISE

Our world needs all the good leaders it can get, so don't be afraid to take a leadership role . . . now.

VERSE 64

All bitterness, anger and wrath,
insult and slander must be removed from you,
along with all wickedness.
And be kind and compassionate to one another,
forgiving one another,
just as God also forgave you in Christ.

Ephesians 4:31-32 Holman CSB

BEYOND BITTERNESS

In the fourth chapter of Ephesians, we are warned about the dangers of bitterness, and with good reason. Bitterness is a spiritual sickness. It will consume your soul; it is dangerous to your emotional health. It can destroy you if you let it . . . so don't let it!

If you are caught up in intense feelings of anger or resentment, you know all too well the destructive power of these emotions. How can you rid yourself of these feelings? First, you must prayerfully ask God to cleanse your heart. Then, you must learn to catch yourself whenever thoughts of bitterness or hatred begin to attack you. Your challenge is this: You must learn to resist negative thoughts before they hijack your emotions.

When you learn to direct your thoughts toward more positive (and rational) topics, you'll be protected from the spiritual and emotional consequences of bitterness . . . and you'll be wiser, healthier, and happier, too. So why wait? Defeat destructive bitterness today.

MORE THOUGHTS ABOUT BITTERNESS

Grudges are like hand grenades; it is wise to release them before they destroy you.

Barbara Johnson

Bitterness is a spiritual cancer, a rapidly growing malignancy that can consume your life. Bitterness cannot be ignored but must be healed at the very core, and only Christ can heal bitterness.

Beth Moore

Sin is any deed or memory that hampers or binds human personality.

Catherine Marshall

Bitterness only makes suffering worse and closes the spiritual channels through which God can pour His grace.

Warren Wiersbe

Forgiveness is the key that unlocks the door of resentment and the handcuffs of hate. It is a power that breaks the chains of bitterness and the shackles of selfishness.

Corrie ten Boom

Forgiveness enables you to bury your grudge in icy earth. To put the past behind you. To flush resentment away by being the first to forgive. Forgiveness fashions your future. It is a brave and brash thing to do.

Barbara Johnson

Bitterness is the greatest barrier to friendship with God.

Rick Warren

Be patient and understanding. Life is too short to be vengeful or malicious.

Phillips Brooks

Bitterness is the trap that snares the hunter.

Max Lucado

A WORD TO THE WISE

You can never fully enjoy the present if you're bitter about the past. Instead of living in the past, make peace with it . . . and move on.

VERSE 65

Do not fear, for I am with you;
do not be afraid, for I am your God.
I will strengthen you; I will help you;
I will hold on to you with My righteous right hand.

Isaiah 41:10 Holman CSB

ABOVE AND BEYOND FEAR

We live in a fear-based world, a world where bad new travels at light speed and good news doesn't. These are troubled times, times when we have legitimate fears for the future of our nation, our world, and our families. But we also have every reason to live courageously. After all, since God has promised to love us and protect us, who—or what—should we fear?

Perhaps you, like countless others, have found your courage tested by the anxieties and fears that are an inevitable part of 21st-century life. If so, let the words of Isaiah 41:10 serve as a reminder that God wants to you to think less about your challenges and more about His love. Remember that He is not just near, He is here, and He's ready to help right now. God will comfort you if you ask Him to. So why not ask? And why not now?

Only believe, don't fear.
Our Master, Jesus, always
watches over us, and no matter
what the persecution,
Jesus will surely overcome it.

Lottie Moon

MORE THOUGHTS ABOUT FEAR

Whether our fear is absolutely realistic or out of proportion in our minds, our greatest refuge is Jesus Christ.

Luci Swindoll

Fear and doubt are conquered by a faith that rejoices. And faith can rejoice because the promises of God are as certain as God Himself.

Kay Arthur

Courage faces fear and thereby masters it. Cowardice represses fear and is thereby mastered by it.

Martin Luther King, Jr.

Our future may look fearfully intimidating, yet we can look up to the Engineer of the Universe, confident that nothing escapes His attention or slips out of the control of those strong hands.

Elisabeth Elliot

A WORD TO THE WISE

Are you feeling anxious or fearful? If so, trust God to handle those problems that are simply too big for you to solve. Entrust the future—your future—to God.

VERSE 66

The one who lives with integrity lives securely,
but whoever perverts his ways will be found out.

Proverbs 10:9 Holman CSB

INTEGRITY MATTERS

Charles Swindoll correctly observed, "Nothing speaks louder or more powerfully than a life of integrity." Godly men and women agree.

Integrity is built slowly over a lifetime. It is the sum of every right decision and every honest word. It is forged on the anvil of honorable work and polished by the twin virtues of honesty and fairness. Integrity is a precious thing—difficult to build but easy to tear down.

As believers in Christ, we must seek to live each day with discipline, honesty, and faith. When we do, at least two things happen: integrity becomes a habit, and God blesses us because of our obedience to Him.

Living a life of integrity isn't always the easiest way, but it is always the right way. God clearly intends that it should be our way, too.

Oswald Chambers, the author of the Christian classic devotional text *My Utmost for His Highest*, advised, "Never support an experience which does not have God as its source, and faith in God as its result." These words serve as a powerful reminder that, as Christians, we are called to walk with God and obey His commandments. But, we live in a world that presents us with countless temptations to stray far from God's path. We Christians, when confronted with sins of any kind, have clear instructions: Walk—or better yet run—in the opposite direction.

It has been said that character is what we are when nobody is watching. How true. When we do things that we know aren't right, we try to hide them from our families and friends. But even if we successfully conceal our sins from the world, we can never conceal our sins from God.

If you sincerely wish to walk with your Creator, follow His commandments. When you do, your character will take care of itself . . . and you won't need to look over your shoulder to see who, besides God, is watching.

The single most important element
in any human relationship is honesty—
with oneself, with God, and with others.

Catherine Marshall

MORE THOUGHTS ABOUT INTEGRITY

God never called us to naïveté. He called us to integrity. The biblical concept of integrity emphasizes mature innocence not childlike ignorance.

Beth Moore

Integrity is the glue that holds our way of life together. We must constantly strive to keep our integrity intact. When wealth is lost, nothing is lost; when health is lost, something is lost; when character is lost, all is lost.

Billy Graham

Honesty has a beautiful and refreshing simplicity about it. No ulterior motives. No hidden meanings. As honesty and integrity characterize our lives, there will be no need to manipulate others.

Charles Swindoll

A WORD TO THE WISE

You children need to hear it from you, so don't hesitate to discuss the importance of honesty. Teach the importance of honesty every day, and, if necessary, use words.

VERSE 67

One thing I do, forgetting those things which are behind and reaching forward to those things which are ahead, I press toward the goal for the prize of the upward call of God in Christ Jesus.

Philippians 3:13-14 NKJV

MAKING PEACE WITH YOUR PAST

Because you are human, you may be slow to forget yesterday's disappointments. But, if you sincerely seek to focus your hopes and energies on the future, then you must find ways to accept the past, no matter how difficult it may be to do so.

In the third chapter of Philippians, Paul tells us that he chose to focus on the future, not the past. Have you made peace with your past? If so, congratulations. But, if you are mired in the quicksand of regret, it's time to plan your escape. How can you do so? By accepting what has been and by trusting God for what will be.

So, Mom, if you have not yet made peace with the past, today is the day to declare an end to all hostilities. When you do, you can then turn your thoughts to the wondrous promises of God and to the glorious future that He has in store for you.

MORE THOUGHTS ABOUT THE PAST

We can't just put our pasts behind us. We've got to put our pasts in front of God.

Beth Moore

Yesterday is just experience but tomorrow is glistening with purpose—and today is the channel leading from one to the other.

Barbara Johnson

Every time the devil reminds you of your past . . . remind him of his future—and yours!

Anonymous

The pages of your past cannot be rewritten, but the pages of your tomorrows are blank.

Zig Ziglar

Whoever you are, whatever your condition or circumstance, whatever your past or problem, Jesus can restore you to wholeness.

Anne Graham Lotz

We set our eyes on the finish line, forgetting the past, and straining toward the mark of spiritual maturity and fruitfulness.

Vonette Bright

The wise man gives proper appreciation in his life to his past. He learns to sift the sawdust of heritage in order to find the nuggets that make the current moment have any meaning.

Grady Nutt

Yesterday ended last night.

John Maxwell

Don't let yesterday use up too much of today.

Dennis Swanberg

A WORD TO THE WISE

The past is past, so don't invest all your energy there. If you're focused on the past, change your focus. If you're living in the past, it's time to stop living there.

VERSE 68

Therefore, get your minds ready for action, being self-disciplined, and set your hope completely on the grace to be brought to you at the revelation of Jesus Christ.

1 Peter 1:13 Holman CSB

THE NEED FOR SELF-DISCIPLINE

God's Word reminds us again and again that our Creator expects us to lead disciplined lives. God doesn't reward laziness, misbehavior, or apathy. To the contrary, He expects us to behave with dignity and discipline. But ours is a world in which dignity and discipline are often in short supply.

We live in a world in which leisure is glorified and indifference is often glamorized. But God has other plans. God gives us talents, and He expects us to use them. But it is not always easy to cultivate those talents. Sometimes, we must invest countless hours (or, in some cases, many years) honing our skills. And that's perfectly okay with God, because He understands that self-discipline is a blessing, not a burden.

Proverbs 23:12 advises: "Apply your heart to discipline And your ears to words of knowledge" (NASB). 2 Peter 1:5-6 teaches, "make every effort to supplement your faith with goodness, goodness with knowledge, knowledge with self-control, self-control with endurance, endurance with godliness" (Holman CSB). Thus, God's Word is clear: we must exercise self-discipline in all matters.

When we pause to consider how much work needs to be done, we realize that self-discipline is not simply a proven way to get ahead; it's also an integral part of God's plan for our lives. If we genuinely seek to be faithful stewards of our time, our talents, and our resources, we must adopt a disciplined approach to life. Otherwise, our talents are wasted and our resources are squandered.

Life's greatest rewards seldom fall into our laps; to the contrary, our greatest accomplishments usually require work, perseverance, and discipline. May we, as disciplined believers, be willing to work for the rewards we so earnestly desire.

You can't climb the ladder of life
with your hands in your pockets.

Barbara Johnson

MORE THOUGHTS ABOUT SELF-DISCIPLINE

"They that sow bountifully shall reap also bountifully," is as true in spiritual things as in material.

Lottie Moon

Obedience to God is our job. The results of that obedience are God's.

Elisabeth Elliot

Simply stated, self-discipline is obedience to God's Word and willingness to submit everything in life to His will, for His ultimate glory.

John MacArthur

As we make an offering of our work, we find the truth of a principle Jesus taught: Fulfillment is not a goal to achieve, but always the by-product of a sacrifice.

Elisabeth Elliot

A WORD TO THE WISE

If you're a disciplined person, you'll earn big rewards. If you're undisciplined, you won't.

VERSE 69

But when the Helper comes,
whom I shall send to you from the Father,
the Spirit of truth who proceeds from the Father,
He will testify of Me.

John 15:26 NKJV

FILLED WITH
THE HOLY SPIRIT

Are you burdened by the pressures of everyday living? If so, it's time to ease the pressure. How can you do it? By allowing the Holy Spirit to fill you and to do His work in your life.

When you are filled with the Holy Spirit, your words and deeds will reflect a love and devotion to God. When you are filled with the Holy Spirit, the steps of your life's journey are guided by the Creator of the universe. When you allow God's Spirit to work in you and through you, you will be energized and transformed.

So today, take God at His word. He has promised to fill you with His Spirit if you let Him. Let Him. And then stand back in amazement as the Father begins to work miracles in your own life and in the lives of those you love.

God wants to teach us that when
we commit our lives to Him,
He gives us that wonderful teacher,
the Holy Spirit.

—

Gloria Gaither

MORE THOUGHTS ABOUT THE HOLY SPIRIT

It is the primary responsibility of the Holy Spirit to glorify Jesus by making us like Him—in our character, in our commitment, and in our communion with the Father.

Anne Graham Lotz

The Holy Spirit will not come to us in his fullness until we see and assent to his priority—his passion for ministry.

Catherine Marshall

The church needs the power and the gifts of the Holy Spirit more now than ever before.

Corrie ten Boom

We have given too much attention to methods and to machinery and to resources, and too little to the Source of Power, the filling with the Holy Ghost.

J. Hudson Taylor

A WORD TO THE WISE

The Holy Spirit is God in us, providing us with all we need to be effective Christians.

On the first day of the week,
very early in the morning, they came to the tomb,
bringing the spices they had prepared.
They found the stone rolled away from the tomb.
They went in but did not find the body of the
Lord Jesus. While they were perplexed about this,
suddenly two men stood by them in dazzling clothes.
So the women were terrified and bowed down
to the ground. "Why are you looking
for the living among the dead?" asked the men.
"He is not here, but He has been resurrected!

Luke 24:1-6 Holman CSB

CONSIDERING THE RESURRECTION

When we consider the resurrection of Christ, we marvel at God's power, His love, and His mercy. And if God is for us, what can we possibly have to fear? The answer, of course, is that those who have been saved by our living Savior have absolutely nothing to fear.

As we consider the meaning of Christ's life, His death, and His resurrection, we are reminded that God's most precious gift, His only Son, went to Calvary as a sacrifice for a sinful world. May we, as believers who have been saved by the blood of Christ, trust the promises of our Savior. And may we honor Him with our words, our deeds, our thoughts, and our prayers—not only today but also throughout all eternity.

MORE THOUGHTS ABOUT THE RESURRECTION

The Resurrection is the biggest news in history. CNN ought to put it on Headline News every thirty minutes. It should scream from every headline: Jesus is alive!

Dennis Swanberg

The resurrection of Jesus Christ is the power of God to change history and to change lives.

Bill Bright

The resurrection of Jesus, the whole alphabet of human hope, the certificate of our Lord's mission from heaven, is the heart of the gospel in all ages.

R. G. Lee

The world has never been stable. Jesus Himself was born into the cruelest and most unstable of worlds. No, we have babies and keep trusting and living because the Resurrection is true! The Resurrection was not just a one-time event in history; it is a principle built into the very fabric of our beings, a fact reverberating from every cell of creation: Life wins! Life wins!

Gloria Gaither

The Resurrection was a proclamation that Christ had conquered sin, death, and the devil. It guarantees there is life beyond the grave.

Charles Stanley

Christ is risen! Hallelujah! / Gladness fills the world today; / From the tomb that could not hold Him, / See, the stone is rolled away!

Fanny Crosby

A WORD TO THE WISE

The resurrection of Jesus is the foundation of the Christian faith—and it should be the foundation of your family's faith, too.

VERSE 71

A word fitly spoken is like
apples of gold in settings of silver.
Proverbs 25:11 NKJV

THE POWER OF WORDS

How important are the words we speak? More important than we may realize. Our words have echoes that extend beyond place or time. If our words are encouraging, we can lift others up; if our words are hurtful, we can hold others back.

So, Mom, here's a question for you and your family to consider: Do you really try to be a source of encouragement to the people you encounter every day? And, are you careful to speak words that lift those people up? If so, you will avoid angry outbursts. You will refrain from impulsive outpourings. You will terminate tantrums. Instead, you will speak words of encouragement and hope to friends, to family members, to coworkers, and even to strangers. And by the way, all the aforementioned people have at least one thing in common: they, like just about everybody else in the world, need all the hope and encouragement they can get.

We will always experience regret
when we live for the moment and
do not weigh our words and deeds
before we give them life.

—

Lisa Bevere

MORE THOUGHTS ABOUT SPEECH

A little kindly advice is better than a great deal of scolding.

Fanny Crosby

When you talk, choose the very same words that you would use if Jesus were looking over your shoulder. Because He is.

Marie T. Freeman

The best use of life is love. The best expression of love is time. The best time to love is now.

Rick Warren

Part of good communication is listening with the eyes as well as with the ears.

Josh McDowell

Attitude and the spirit in which we communicate are as important as the words we say.

Charles Stanley

A WORD TO THE WISE

You can guard your heart by paying careful attention to the words you speak. So measure your words carefully and prayerfully.

VERSE 72

The one who conceals his sins will not prosper,
but whoever confesses and
renounces them will find mercy.

Proverbs 28:13 Holman CSB

WHEN YOU MAKE A MISTAKE

Everybody makes mistakes, and so will you. In fact, Winston Churchill once observed, "Success is going from failure to failure without loss of enthusiasm." What was good for Churchill is also good for you. You should expect to make mistakes—plenty of mistakes—but you should not allow those missteps to rob you of the enthusiasm you need to fulfill God's plan for your life.

We are imperfect people living in an imperfect world; mistakes are simply part of the price we pay for being here. But, even though mistakes are an inevitable part of life's journey, repeated mistakes should not be. When we commit the inevitable blunders of life, we must correct them, learn from them, and pray for the wisdom not to repeat them. When we do, our mistakes become lessons, and our lives become adventures in growth, not stagnation.

Have you made a mistake or three? Of course you have. But here's the big question: have you used your mistakes as stumbling blocks or stepping stones? The answer to that question will determine how well you will perform in the workplace and in every other aspect of your life.

MORE THOUGHTS ABOUT MISTAKES

Sin is largely a matter of mistaken priorities. Any sin in us that is cherished, hidden, and not confessed will cut the nerve center of our faith.

Catherine Marshall

God is able to take mistakes, when they are committed to Him, and make of them something for our good and for His glory.

Ruth Bell Graham

One of the ways God refills us after failure is through the blessing of Christian fellowship. Just experiencing the joy of simple activities shared with other children of God can have a healing effect on us.

Anne Graham Lotz

In essence, my testimony is that there is life after failure: abundant, effective, spirit-filled life for those who are willing to repent hard and work hard.

Beth Moore

A live body is not one that never gets hurt, but one that can to some extent repair itself. In the same way a Christian is not a man who never goes wrong, but a man who is enabled to repent and pick himself up and begin over again after each stumble—because the Christ-life is inside him, repairing him all the time, enabling him to repeat (in some degree) the kind of voluntary death which Christ himself carried out.

C. S. Lewis

Truth will sooner come out of error than from confusion.

Francis Bacon

Mistakes offer the possibility for redemption and a new start in God's kingdom. No matter what you're guilty of, God can restore your innocence.

Barbara Johnson

A WORD TO THE WISE

It is not a sign of weakness when you apologize to your child. If you make a mistake, say so. When you do, your child will learn a valuable lesson.

VERSE 73

*Commit your activities to the Lord
and your plans will be achieved.*

Proverbs 16:3 Holman CSB

DEFINING SUCCESS

How do you define success? Do you define it as the accumulation of material possessions or the adulation of your neighbors? If so, you need to reorder your priorities. Genuine success has little to do with fame or fortune; it has everything to do with God's gift of love and His promise of salvation.

If you have accepted Christ as your personal Savior, you are already a towering success in the eyes of God, but there is still more that you can do. Your task—as a believer who has been touched by the Creator's grace—is to accept the spiritual abundance and peace that He offers through the person of His Son. Then, you can share the healing message of God's love and His abundance with a world that desperately needs both. When you do, you have reached the pinnacle of success.

God provides the ingredients
for our daily bread
but expects us to do the baking.
With our own hands!

—

Barbara Johnson

MORE THOUGHTS ABOUT SUCCESS

Winners see an answer for every problem; losers see a problem in every answer.

Barbara Johnson

In essence, my testimony is that there is life after failure: abundant, effective, spirit-filled life for those who are willing to repent hard and work hard.

Beth Moore

There's not much you can't achieve or endure if you know God is walking by your side. Just remember: Someone knows, and Someone cares.

Bill Hybels

We, as believers, must allow God to define success. And, when we do, God blesses us with His love and His grace.

Jim Gallery

A WORD TO THE WISE

Don't let the world define success for you. Only God can do that.

Do not be deceived:
"Bad company corrupts good morals."

1 Corinthians 15:33 Holman CSB

FOLLOWING GOD, NOT "THE CROWD"

Rick Warren observed, "Those who follow the crowd usually get lost in it." We know those words to be true, but oftentimes we fail to live by them. Instead of trusting God for guidance, we imitate our friends and suffer the consequences. Instead of seeking to please our Father in heaven, we strive to please our peers, with decidedly mixed results. Instead of doing the right thing, we do the "easy" thing or the "popular" thing. And when we do, we pay a high price for our shortsightedness.

Would you like a time-tested formula for successful living? Here is a simple formula that is proven and true: don't give in to peer pressure. Period.

Instead of getting lost in the crowd, you should find guidance from God. Does this sound too simple? Perhaps it is simple, but it is also the only way to reap all the marvelous riches that God has in store for you.

MORE THOUGHTS ABOUT PEER PRESSURE

For better or worse, you will eventually become more and more like the people you associate with. So why not associate with people who make you better, not worse?

Marie T. Freeman

It is comfortable to know that we are responsible to God and not to man. It is a small matter to be judged of man's judgement.

Lottie Moon

We, as God's people, are not only to stay far away from sin and sinners who would entice us, but we are to be so like our God that we mourn over sin.

Kay Arthur

Comparison is the root of all feelings of inferiority.

James Dobson

It's tempting to follow the crowd, but usually it's better to follow your conscience.

Criswell Freeman

Do you want to be wise? Choose wise friends.

Charles Swindoll

Ambition! We must be careful what we mean by it. If it means the desire to get ahead of other people—which is what I think it does mean—then it is bad. If it simply means wanting to do a thing well, then it is good. It isn't wrong for an actor to want to act his part as well as it can possibly be acted, but the wish to have his name in bigger type than the other actors is a bad one.

C. S. Lewis

Those who follow the crowd usually get lost in it.

Rick Warren

You will get untold flak for prioritizing God's revealed and present will for your life over man's . . . but, boy, is it worth it.

Beth Moore

Fashion is an enduring testimony to the fact that we live quite consciously before the eyes of others.

John Eldredge

A WORD TO THE WISE

A great way to guard your steps is by associating with friends who guard theirs.

So he who had received five talents came
and brought five other talents, saying,
"Lord, you delivered to me five talents;
look, I have gained five more talents besides them."
His lord said to him, "Well done, good and faithful
servant; you were faithful over a few things,
I will make you ruler over many things.
Enter into the joy of your lord."

Matthew 25:20-21 NKJV

USING YOUR TALENTS

The old saying is both familiar and true: "What we are is God's gift to us; what we become is our gift to God." Each of us possesses special talents, gifted by God, that can be nurtured carefully or ignored totally. Our challenge, of course, is to use our abilities to the greatest extent possible and to use them in ways that honor our Savior.

Are you using your natural talents to make God's world a better place? If so, congratulations. But if you have gifts that you have not fully explored and developed, perhaps you need to have a chat with the One who gave you those gifts in the first place. Your talents are priceless treasures offered from your Heavenly Father. Use them. After all, an obvious way to say "thank You" to the Giver is to use the gifts He has given.

In the great orchestra we call life,
you have an instrument and a song,
and you owe it to God
to play them both sublimely.

Max Lucado

MORE THOUGHTS ABOUT TALENTS

Not everyone possesses boundless energy or a conspicuous talent. We are not equally blessed with great intellect or physical beauty or emotional strength. But we have all been given the same ability to be faithful.

Gigi Graham Tchividjian

What we are is God's gift to us. What we become is our gift to God.

Anonymous

You are a unique blend of talents, skills, and gifts, which makes you an indispensable member of the body of Christ.

Charles Stanley

God often reveals His direction for our lives through the way He made us . . . with a certain personality and unique skills.

Bill Hybels

A WORD TO THE WISE

God has given you a unique array of talents and opportunities. The rest is up to you.

*Pride goes before destruction,
and a haughty spirit before a fall.*

Proverbs 16:18 NKJV

BEWARE OF PRIDE

The words from Proverbs 16 remind us that pride and destruction are traveling partners. But as imperfect human beings, we are tempted to puff out our chests and crow about our own accomplishments. When we do so, we delude ourselves.

As Christians, we have a profound reason to be humble: We have been refashioned and saved by Jesus Christ, and that salvation came not because of our own good works but because of God's grace. Thus, we are not "self-made"; we are "God-made" and "Christ-saved." How, then, can we be boastful? The answer, of course, is simple: if we are honest with ourselves and with our God, we cannot be boastful. In the quiet moments, when we search the depths of our own hearts, we know that whatever "it" is, God did that. And He deserves the credit.

MORE THOUGHTS ABOUT PRIDE

That's what I love about serving God. In His eyes, there are no little people . . . because there are no big people. We are all on the same playing field. We all start at square one. No one has it better than the other, or possesses unfair advantage.

Joni Eareckson Tada

We cannot be filled until we are empty. We have to be poor in spirit of ourselves in order to be filled with the Holy Spirit.

Corrie ten Boom

All kindness and good deeds, we must keep silent. The result will be an inner reservoir of personal power.

Catherine Marshall

There is nothing so natural to man, nothing so insidious and hidden from our sight, nothing so difficult and dangerous, as pride.

Andrew Murray

Jesus had a humble heart. If He abides in us, pride will never dominate our lives.

Billy Graham

Humility is a thing which must be genuine; the imitation of it is the nearest thing in the world to pride.

C. H. Spurgeon

When you have good, healthy relationships with your family and friends you're more prompted to laugh and not take yourself so seriously.

Dennis Swanberg

It was as important to me that my children be no more self-righteous than they were unrighteous. In His Gospels, Christ seemed far more tolerant of a repentant sinner than a self-righteous, self-proclaimed saint.

Beth Moore

Our Lord did not say it was wrong to pray in the corners of the street, but He did say it was wrong to have the motive to "be seen of men."

Oswald Chambers

A WORD TO THE WISE

All of your talents and abilities come from God. Give Him thanks, and give Him the glory.

VERSE 77

If we confess our sins,
He is faithful and righteous to forgive us our sins
and to cleanse us from all unrighteousness.

1 John 1:9 Holman CSB

REAL REPENTANCE

All of us (even "almost perfect" parents) have made mistakes, sometimes BIG mistakes. And when we fall short of our own expectations, or God's, we may experience intense feelings of guilt. But God has an answer for the guilt that we feel. That answer, of course, is His forgiveness. When we confess our mistakes, if we learn from them, and if we stop repeating them, then we have every right to forgive ourselves.

Are you troubled by feelings of guilt or regret? If so, you must put yourself back on the right path (by putting an end to your misbehavior), and you must ask your Heavenly Father for His forgiveness. When you do, He will forgive you completely and without reservation. Then, you must forgive yourself just as God has forgiven you: thoroughly and unconditionally.

Full and true repentance is
literally an about-face.
It means turning
completely around, away from sin,
and turning toward God.

—

Shirley Dobson

More Thoughts About Repentance

Four marks of true repentance are: acknowledgement of wrong, willingness to confess it, willingness to abandon it, and willingness to make restitution.

Corrie ten Boom

God sees everything we've ever done and He's willing to forgive. But we must confess to Him.

Ruth Bell Graham

We have a decision to make—to turn away from sin or to be miserable and suffer the consequences of continual disobedience.

Vonette Bright

Real repentance is always accompanied by godly sorrow. Asking God to forgive us for a sin we are not yet sorry we committed is a waste of time.

Beth Moore

A Word to the Wise

If you're engaged in behavior that is displeasing to God, repent today—tomorrow may be too late.

VERSE 78

Be an example to the believers in word,
in conduct, in love, in spirit, in faith, in purity.

1 Timothy 4:12 NKJV

BEING THE RIGHT KIND OF EXAMPLE

Our children learn from the lessons we teach and the lives we live, but not necessarily in that order. As mothers, we serve as unforgettable role models for our children and grandchildren. Hopefully, the lives we lead and the choices we make will serve as enduring examples of the spiritual abundance that is available to all who worship God and obey His commandments.

What kind of example are you? Are you the kind of mother whose life serves as a genuine example of patience and righteousness? Are you a woman whose behavior serves as a positive role model for others? Are you the kind of mom whose actions, day in and day out, are based upon kindness, faithfulness, and a sincere love for the Lord? If so, you are not only blessed by God, but you are also a powerful force for good in a world that desperately needs positive influences such as yours.

Corrie ten Boom advised, "Don't worry about what you do not understand. Worry about what you do understand in the Bible but do not live by." And that's sound advice because our families and friends are watching . . . and so, for that matter, is God.

MORE THOUGHTS ABOUT SETTING THE RIGHT KIND OF EXAMPLE

Among the most joyful people I have known have been some who seem to have had no human reason for joy. The sweet fragrance of Christ has shown through their lives.

Elisabeth Elliot

In serving we uncover the greatest fulfillment within and become a stellar example of a woman who knows and loves Jesus.

Vonette Bright

Your life is destined to be an example. The only question is "what kind?"

Marie T. Freeman

We must mirror God's love in the midst of a world full of hatred. We are the mirrors of God's love, so we may show Jesus by our lives.

Corrie ten Boom

Each one of us is God's special work of art. Through us, He teaches and inspires, delights and encourages, informs and uplifts all those who view our lives. God, the master artist, is most concerned about expressing Himself—His thoughts and His intentions—through what He paints in our character . . . . [He] wants to paint a beautiful portrait of His Son in and through your life. A painting like no other in all of time.

Joni Eareckson Tada

Integrity of heart is indispensable.

John Calvin

If I take care of my character, my reputation will take care of itself.

D. L. Moody

There is no way to grow a saint overnight. Character, like the oak tree, does not spring up like a mushroom.

Vance Havner

A WORD TO THE WISE

Live according to the principles you teach. The sermons you live are far more important than the sermons you preach.

VERSE 79

Now godliness with contentment is great gain.
For we brought nothing into this world,
and it is certain we can carry nothing out.
And having food and clothing,
with these we shall be content.

1 Timothy 6:6-8 NKJV

KEEP IT SIMPLE

You live in a world where simplicity is in short supply. Think for a moment about the complexity of your everyday life and compare it to the lives of your ancestors. Certainly, you are the beneficiary of many technological innovations, but those innovations have a price: in all likelihood, your world is highly complex. Consider the following:

1. From the moment you wake up in the morning until the time you lay your head on the pillow at night, you are the target of an endless stream of advertising information. Each message is intended to grab your attention in order to convince you to purchase things you didn't know you needed (and probably don't!).

2. Essential aspects of your life, including personal matters such as health care, are subject to an ever-increasing flood of rules and regulations.

3. Unless you take firm control of your time and your life, you may be overwhelmed by an ever-increasing tidal wave of complexity that threatens your happiness.

Your Heavenly Father understands the joy of living simply, and so should you. So do yourself a favor: keep your life as simple as possible. Simplicity is, indeed, genius. By simplifying your life, you are destined to improve it.

MORE THOUGHTS ABOUT SIMPLICITY

Prescription for a happier and healthier life: resolve to slow down your pace; learn to say no gracefully; resist the temptation to chase after more pleasure, more hobbies, and more social entanglements.

James Dobson

There is absolutely no evidence that complexity and materialism lead to happiness. On the contrary, there is plenty of evidence that simplicity and spirituality lead to joy, a blessedness that is better than happiness.

Dennis Swanberg

A peaceful heart finds joy in all of life's simple pleasures.

Anonymous

We Christians must simplify our lives or lose untold treasures on earth and in eternity. Modern civilization is so complex as to make the devotional life all but impossible. The need for solitude and quietness was never greater than it is today.

A. W. Tozer

Efficiency is enhanced not by what we accomplish but more often by what we relinquish.

Charles Swindoll

Among the enemies to devotion, none is so harmful as distractions. Whatever excites the curiosity, scatters the thoughts, disquiets the heart, absorbs the interests, or shifts our life focus from the kingdom of God within us to the world around us—that is a distraction; and the world is full of them.

A. W. Tozer

A WORD TO THE WISE

Simplicity and peace are two concepts that are closely related. Complexity and peace are not.

VERSE 80

Draw near to God,
and He will draw near to you.

James 4:8 Holman CSB

DRAW NEAR TO GOD

If God is everywhere, why does He sometimes seem so far away? The answer to that question, of course, has nothing to do with God and everything to do with us.

When we begin each day on our knees, in praise and worship to Him, God often seems very near indeed. But, if we ignore God's presence or—worse yet—rebel against it altogether, the world in which we live becomes a spiritual wasteland.

Are you tired, discouraged, or fearful? Be comforted because God is with you. Are you confused? Listen to the quiet voice of your Heavenly Father. Are you bitter? Talk with God and seek His guidance. Are you celebrating a great victory? Thank God and praise Him. He is the Giver of all things good.

In whatever condition you find yourself, wherever you are, whether you are happy or sad, victorious or vanquished, troubled or triumphant, celebrate God's presence. And be comforted. God is not just near; He has promised that He is right here, right now. And that's a promise you can depend on.

MORE THOUGHTS ABOUT GOD'S PRESENCE

As God perfects us, He keeps us protected from the pride that might otherwise develop by veiling, to some extent, our progress in our own eyes. The light of the glory of His presence shines two ways: it sheds light on the knowledge of God so that we can learn to see Him more clearly, but it also sheds light on ourselves so that we can see our own sin more clearly.

Beth Moore

If you want to hear God's voice clearly and you are uncertain, then remain in His presence until He changes that uncertainty. Often, much can happen during this waiting for the Lord. Sometimes, He changes pride into humility, doubt into faith and peace.

Corrie ten Boom

God walks with us. He scoops us up in His arms or simply sits with us in silent strength until we cannot avoid the awesome recognition that yes, even now, He is here.

Gloria Gaither

If your heart has grown cold, it is because you have moved away from the fire of His presence.

Beth Moore

Make the least of all that goes and the most of all that comes. Don't regret what is past. Cherish what you have. Look forward to all that is to come. And most important of all, rely moment by moment on Jesus Christ.

Gigi Graham Tchividjian

A sense of deity is inscribed on every heart.

John Calvin

The next time you hear a baby laugh or see an ocean wave, take note. Pause and listen as His Majesty whispers ever so gently, "I'm here."

Max Lucado

A WORD TO THE WISE

God isn't far away—He's right here, right now. And He's willing to talk to you right here, right now.

The borrower is servant to the lender.

Proverbs 22:7 NIV

BEWARE OF DEBT

We live in a world that is addicted to debt, but you needn't be. Just because our world revolves around borrowed money doesn't mean that you must do likewise.

If you're already living beyond your means and borrowing to pay for the privilege, then you know that sleepless nights and stress-filled days are the psychological payments that must be extracted from those who buy too much "now" in hopes that they can pay for those things "later." Unfortunately, "later" usually arrives sooner than expected, and that's when the trouble begins.

Whether you're buying a mattress, a microwave, or a Maserati, somebody will probably be willing to sell it to you on credit. But the Bible makes it clear that the instant you become a debtor, you also become a servant to the lender. So if you're trying to decide whether or not to make that next big purchase, remember that when it comes to borrowed money, less is usually more . . . much more.

Having money
may not make people happy,
but owing money
is sure to make them miserable.

—

John Maxwell

MORE THOUGHTS ABOUT DEBT

Getting out of the pit requires we surround ourselves with people who love us enough to support us and lift us up when we are at our ugliest.

Dave Ramsey

God says that when you borrow, you become a servant of the lender; the lender is established as an authority over the borrower. (Proverbs 22:7)

Larry Burkett

Nobody is going to simplify your life for you. You've got to simplify things for yourself.

Marie T. Freeman

Getting out of the pit requires we surround ourselves with people who love us enough to support us and lift us up when we are at our ugliest.

Dave Ramsey

A WORD TO THE WISE

Nothing is more dangerous to your financial health than the undisciplined use of credit. Don't borrow money for things that go down in value, and if you can't use credit cards responsibly, cut them up.

VERSE 82

He did it with all his heart. So he prospered.
2 Chronicles 31:21 NKJV

PUTTING YOUR HEART INTO YOUR WORK

The old adage is both familiar and true: We must pray as if everything depended upon God but work as if everything depended upon us. Yet sometimes, when we are weary and discouraged, we may allow our worries to sap our energy and our hope. God has other intentions. God intends that we pray for things, and He intends that we be willing to work for the things that we pray for. More importantly, God intends that our work should become His work.

Whether you're at home or in the workplace, your success will depend, in large part, upon the passion that you bring to your work. God did not create you for a life of mediocrity; He created you for far greater things. Reaching for greater things usually requires work and lots of it, which is perfectly fine with God. After all, He knows that you're up to the task, and He has big plans for you. Very big plans . . .

Life is too short to spend it
being angry, bored, or dull.

—

Barbara Johnson

MORE THOUGHTS ABOUT PASSION

If your heart has grown cold, it is because you have moved away from the fire of His presence.

Beth Moore

Success or failure can be pretty well predicted by the degree to which the heart is fully in it.

John Eldredge

We honor God by asking for great things when they are part of His promise. We dishonor Him and cheat ourselves when we ask for molehills where He has offered mountains.

Vance Havner

One of the great needs in the church today is for every Christian to become enthusiastic about his faith in Jesus Christ.

Billy Graham

A WORD TO THE WISE

When you are passionate about your life and your faith . . . great things happen.

VERSE 83

In fact, when we were with you,
this is what we commanded you:
"If anyone isn't willing to work, he should not eat."

2 Thessalonians 3:10 Holman CSB

WE'RE EXPECTED TO WORK

God's Word teaches us the value of hard work. In his second letter to the Thessalonians, Paul warns, "If anyone isn't willing to work, he should not eat." And the Book of Proverbs proclaims, "One who is slack in his work is brother to one who destroys" (18:9 NIV). In short, God has created a world in which diligence is rewarded but sloth is not. So, whatever it is that you choose to do, do it with commitment, excitement, and vigor.

Hard work is not simply a proven way to get ahead; it's also part of God's plan for you. God did not create you for a life of mediocrity; He created you for far greater things. Reaching for greater things usually requires work and lots of it, which is perfectly fine with God. After all, He knows that you're up to the task, and He has big plans for you if you possess a loving heart and willing hands.

We must trust as if
it all depended on God
and work as if
it all depended on us.

—

C. H. Spurgeon

MORE THOUGHTS ABOUT WORK

Ordinary work, which is what most of us do most of the time, is ordained by God every bit as much as is the extraordinary.

Elisabeth Elliot

Great relief and satisfaction can come from seeking God's priorities for us in each season, discerning what is "best" in the midst of many noble opportunities, and pouring our most excellent energies into those things.

Beth Moore

In the very place where God has put us, whatever its limitations, whatever kind of work it may be, we may indeed serve the Lord Christ.

Elisabeth Elliot

If you honor God with your work, He will honor you because of your work.

Marie T. Freeman

A WORD TO THE WISE

When you find work that pleases God—and when you apply yourself conscientiously to the job at hand—you'll be rewarded.

VERSE 84

Therefore, if anyone is in Christ,
he is a new creation; old things have passed away;
behold, all things have become new.

2 Corinthians 5:17 NKJV

THE NEW YOU

In 2 Corinthians 5:17, we are told that when a person accepts Christ, he or she becomes a new creation. Have you invited God's Son to reign over your heart and your life? If so, think for a moment about the "old" you, the person you were before you invited Christ into your heart. Now, think about the "new" you, the person you have become since then. Is there a difference between the "old" you and the "new and improved" version? There should be! And that difference should be noticeable not only to you but also to others.

Warren Wiersbe observed, "The greatest miracle of all is the transformation of a lost sinner into a child of God." And Oswald Chambers noted, "If the Spirit of God has transformed you within, you will exhibit Divine characteristics in your life, not good human characteristics. God's life in us expresses itself as God's life, not as a human life trying to be godly."

When you invited Christ to reign over your heart, you became a new creation through Him. This day offers yet another opportunity to behave yourself like that new creation by serving your Creator and strengthening your character. When you do, God will guide your steps and bless your endeavors today and forever.

MORE THOUGHTS ABOUT CONVERSION

The amazing thing about Jesus is that He doesn't just patch up our lives; He gives us a brand new sheet, a clean slate to start over, all new.

Gloria Gaither

Be filled with the Holy Spirit; join a church where the members believe the Bible and know the Lord; seek the fellowship of other Christians; learn and be nourished by God's Word and His many promises. Conversion is not the end of your journey—it is only the beginning.

Corrie ten Boom

If we accept His invitation to salvation, we live with Him forever. However, if we do not accept because we refuse His only Son as our Savior, then we exclude ourselves from My Father's House. It's our choice.

Anne Graham Lotz

If you are God's child, you are no longer bound to your past or to what you were. You are a brand new creature in Christ Jesus.

Kay Arthur

Being born again is God's solution to our need for love and life and light.

Anne Graham Lotz

God is not a supernatural interferer; God is the everlasting portion of his people. When a man born from above begins his new life, he meets God at every turn, hears him in every sound, sleeps at his feet, and wakes to find him there.

Oswald Chambers

Has he taken over your heart? Perhaps he resides there, but does he preside there?

Vance Havner

A WORD TO THE WISE

Unless you're a radically different person because of your relationship with Jesus, your faith isn't what it could be . . . or should be.

Give thanks to the Lord,
for He is good;
His faithful love endures forever.

Psalm 106:1 Holman CSB

HE LOVED US FIRST

As a mother, you know the profound love that you hold in your heart for your own children. As a child of God, you can only imagine the infinite love that your Heavenly Father holds for you.

God made you in His own image and gave you salvation through the person of His Son Jesus Christ. And now, precisely because you are a wondrous creation treasured by God, a question presents itself: What will you do in response to the Creator's love? Will you ignore it or embrace it? Will you return it or neglect it? That decision, of course, is yours and yours alone.

When you embrace God's love, you are forever changed. When you embrace God's love, you feel differently about yourself, your neighbors, your family, and your world. More importantly, you share God's message— and His love—with others.

Your Heavenly Father—a God of infinite love and mercy—is waiting to embrace you with open arms. Accept His love today and forever.

I love Him because He first loved me,
and He still does love me,
and He will love me forever and ever.

Bill Bright

MORE THOUGHTS ABOUT GOD'S LOVE

The fact is, God no longer deals with us in judgment but in mercy. If people got what they deserved, this old planet would have ripped apart at the seams centuries ago. Praise God that because of His great love "we are not consumed, for his compassions never fail" (Lam. 3:22).

Joni Eareckson Tada

Being loved by Him whose opinion matters most gives us the security to risk loving, too—even loving ourselves.

Gloria Gaither

There is no pit so deep that God's love is not deeper still.

Corrie ten Boom

I think God knew that the message we sometimes need to hear today is not what a great and mighty God we serve, but rather what a tender, loving Father we have, even when He says no.

Lisa Whelchel

A WORD TO THE WISE

When all else fails, God's love does not. You can always depend upon God's love . . . and He is always your ultimate protection.

No temptation has overtaken you
except such as is common to man;
but God is faithful, who will not allow you
to be tempted beyond what you are able,
but with the temptation will also make
the way of escape, that you may be able to bear it.

1 Corinthians 10:13 NKJV

RESISTING TEMPTATION

It's inevitable: today you will be tempted by somebody or something—in fact, you will probably be tempted many times. Why? Because you live in a world that is filled to the brim with temptations! Some of these temptations are small; eating a second scoop of ice cream, for example, is enticing but not very dangerous. Other temptations, however, are not nearly so harmless.

The devil is working 24/7, and he's causing pain and heartache in more ways than ever before. We, as believers, must remain watchful and strong. And the good news is this: When it comes to fighting Satan, we are never alone. God is always with us, and He gives us the power to resist temptation whenever we ask Him to give us strength.

In a letter to believers, Peter offered a stern warning: "Your adversary, the devil, prowls around like a roaring lion, seeking someone to devour" (1 Peter 5:8 NASB). As Christians, we must take that warning seriously, and we must behave accordingly.

Flee temptation
without leaving a forwarding address.

Barbara Johnson

MORE THOUGHTS ABOUT TEMPTATION

There is sharp necessity for giving Christ absolute obedience. The devil bids for our complete self-will. To whatever extent we give this self-will the right to be master over our lives, we are, to an extent, giving Satan a toehold.

Catherine Marshall

Instant intimacy is one of the leading warning signals of a seduction.

Beth Moore

Lord, what joy to know that Your powers are so much greater than those of the enemy.

Corrie ten Boom

Deception is the enemy's ongoing plan of attack.

Stormie Omartian

It is easier to stay out of temptation than to get out of it.

Rick Warren

A WORD TO THE WISE

Because you live in a temptation-filled world, you must guard your eyes, your thoughts, and your heart—all day, every day.

VERSE 87

*But this I say: He who sows sparingly
will also reap sparingly, and he who sows bountifully
will also reap bountifully. So let each one give as he
purposes in his heart, not grudgingly or of necessity;
for God loves a cheerful giver.*

2 Corinthians 9:6-7 NKJV

GENEROSITY NOW

Are you a cheerful giver? If you're a mom who's intent upon obeying God's commandments, you must be. When you give, God looks not only at the quality of your gift, but also at the condition of your heart. If you give generously, joyfully, and without complaint, you obey God's Word. But, if you make your gifts grudgingly, or if the motivation for your gift is selfish, you disobey your Creator, even if you have tithed in accordance with Biblical principles.

In 2 Corinthians 9, Paul reminds us that when we sow the seeds of generosity, we reap bountiful rewards in accordance with God's plan for our lives. Thus, we are instructed to give cheerfully and without reservation.

So today, Mom, take God's instructions to heart and make this pledge to yourself and your Creator: Vow to be a cheerful, generous, courageous giver. The world needs your help, and you need the spiritual rewards that will be yours when you give faithfully, prayerfully, cheerfully . . . and often.

MORE THOUGHTS ABOUT GENEROSITY

The measure of a life, after all, is not its duration but its donation.

Corrie ten Boom

Here lies the tremendous mystery—that God should be all-powerful, yet refuse to coerce. He summons us to cooperation. We are honored in being given the opportunity to participate in his good deeds. Remember how He asked for help in performing His miracles: Fill the water pots, stretch out your hand, distribute the loaves.

Elisabeth Elliot

What is your focus today? Joy comes when it is Jesus first, others second . . . then you.

Kay Arthur

God does not need our money. But, you and I need the experience of giving it.

James Dobson

The happiest and most joyful people are those who give money and serve.

Dave Ramsey

When somebody needs a helping hand, he doesn't need it tomorrow or the next day. He needs it now, and that's exactly when you should offer to help. Good deeds, if they are really good, happen sooner rather than later.

Marie T. Freeman

God does not supply money to satisfy our every whim and desire. His promise is to meet our needs and provide an abundance so that we can help other people.

Larry Burkett

We are never more like God than when we give.

Charles Swindoll

A WORD TO THE WISE

It's never too early to emphasize the importance of giving. From the time that a child is old enough to drop a penny into the offering plate, we, as parents, should stress the obligation that we all have to share the blessings that God has shared with us.

*Should we accept only good from God
and not adversity?*

Job 2:10 Holman CSB

LEARNING THE ART OF ACCEPTANCE

I f you're like most people, you like being in control. Period. You want things to happen according to your wishes and according to your timetable. But sometimes, God has other plans . . . and He always has the final word. Job understood the importance of accepting God's sovereignty in good times and bad . . . and so should you.

The American theologian Reinhold Niebuhr composed a profoundly simple verse that came to be known as the Serenity Prayer: "God, grant me the serenity to accept the things I cannot change, the courage to change the things I can, and the wisdom to know the difference." Niebuhr's words are far easier to recite than they are to live by.

Oswald Chambers correctly observed, "Our Lord never asks us to decide for Him; He asks us to yield to Him—a very different matter." These words remind us that even when we cannot understand the workings of God, we must trust Him and accept His will.

Are you embittered by a personal tragedy that you did not deserve and cannot understand? If so, it's time to make peace with life. It's time to forgive others, and, if necessary, to forgive yourself. It's time to accept the unchangeable past, to embrace the priceless present, and to have faith in the promise of tomorrow. It's time to trust God completely. And it's time to reclaim the peace—His peace—that can and should be yours.

So if you've encountered unfortunate circumstances that are beyond your power to control, accept those circumstances . . . and trust God. When you do, you can be comforted in the knowledge that your Creator is both loving and wise, and that He understands His plans perfectly, even when you do not.

Ultimately things work out best
for those who make the best
of the way things work out.

Barbara Johnson

MORE THOUGHTS ABOUT ACCEPTANCE

When we face an impossible situation, all self-reliance and self-confidence must melt away; we must be totally dependent on Him for the resources.

Anne Graham Lotz

I have held many things in my hands, and I have lost them all; but whatever I have placed in God's hands, that I still possess.

Corrie ten Boom

Acceptance says: True, this is my situation at the moment. I'll look unblinkingly at the reality of it. But, I'll also open my hands to accept willingly whatever a loving Father sends me.

Catherine Marshall

I am truly grateful that faith enables me to move past the question of "Why?"

Zig Ziglar

A WORD TO THE WISE

When you encounter situations that you cannot change, you must learn the wisdom of acceptance . . . and you must learn to trust God.

VERSE 89

But be doers of the word,
and not hearers only, deceiving yourselves.

James 1:22 NKJV

ACTIONS SPEAK LOUDER

The old saying is both familiar and true: actions speak louder than words. And as believers, we must beware: our actions should always give credence to the changes that Christ can make in the lives of those who walk with Him.

God calls upon each of us to act in accordance with His will and with respect for His commandments. If we are to be responsible believers, we must realize that it is never enough simply to hear the instructions of God; we must also live by them. And it is never enough to wait idly by while others do God's work here on earth; we, too, must act. Doing God's work is a responsibility that each of us must bear, and when we do, our loving Heavenly Father rewards our efforts with a bountiful harvest.

Do you seek God's peace and His blessings? Then obey Him. When you're faced with a difficult choice or a powerful temptation, seek God's counsel and trust the counsel He gives. Invite God into your heart and act in accordance with His commandments. When you do, Mom, you will be blessed today, tomorrow, and forever.

MORE THOUGHTS ABOUT TAKING ACTION NOW

Never fail to do something because you don't feel like it. Sometimes you just have to do it now, and you'll feel like it later.

Marie T. Freeman

From the very moment one feels called to act is born the strength to bear whatever horror one will feel or see. In some inexplicable way, terror loses its overwhelming power when it becomes a task that must be faced.

Emmi Bonhoeffer

A bird does not know it can fly before it uses its wings. We learn God's love in our hearts as soon as we act upon it.

Corrie ten Boom

We spend our lives dreaming of the future, not realizing that a little of it slips away every day.

Barbara Johnson

We set the sail; God makes the wind.

Anonymous

Logic will not change an emotion, but action will.

Zig Ziglar

It's sobering, it's shocking, it's almost beyond belief, but it is 100 percent biblically true: Every one of our actions and attitudes affects God. By His nature He is an expressive God, and He has given us the capability of stirring His heart.

Bill Hybels

The church needs people who are doers of the Word and not just hearers.

Warren Wiersbe

Do noble things, do not dream them all day long.

Charles Kingsley

Paul did one thing. Most of us dabble in forty things. Are you a doer or a dabbler?

Vance Havner

A WORD TO THE WISE

Because actions do speak louder than words, it's always a good time to let your actions speak for themselves.

VERSE 90

So then, they are no longer two but one flesh.
Therefore what God has joined together,
let not man separate.

Matthew 19:6 NKJV

ABOUT MARRIAGE

L ove is a journey. A healthy marriage is a lifelong exercise in love, fidelity, trust, understanding, forgiveness, caring, sharing, and encouragement. It requires empathy, tenderness, patience, and perseverance. It is the union of two adults, both of whom are willing to compromise and, when appropriate, to apologize. It requires heaping helpings of common sense, common courtesy, and uncommon caring. A healthy marriage is a joy to behold, an even greater joy to experience . . . and a blessing forever.

The loving relationship between a husband and wife may require the couple to travel together through the dark valleys of disappointment and sorrow, but even on those darkest days, the couple can remain steadfast . . . if they choose to follow God.

When we behave ourselves as obedient servants, we honor the Father and the Son. When we live righteously and according to God's commandments, we build better marriages and better lives. When we obey God, He blesses us in ways that we cannot fully understand. So, as this day unfolds, take every step of your journey with God as your traveling companion. Study His Holy Word. Follow His commandments. Support only those activities that further God's kingdom and your spiritual growth. Be an example of righteous living to your neighbors, to your children, and to your spouse. And make certain that you keep God where He belongs: at the center of all your relationships, including your marriage.

A marriage can't survive forever on leftovers.
It needs to be fed continually,
or it will eventually starve.

John Maxwell

MORE THOUGHTS ABOUT MARRIAGE

Both a good marriage and a bad marriage have moments of struggle, but in a healthy relationship, the husband and wife search for answers and areas of agreement because they love each other.

James Dobson

A Christian wife's responsibility balances delicately between knowing when to submit and when to outwit. Adapting to our husbands never implies the annihilation of our creativity, rather the blossoming of it.

Ruth Bell Graham

How committed are you to breaking the ice of prayer-lessness so that you and your mate can seek the Lord openly and honestly together, releasing control over your marriage into the capable, trustworthy, but often surprising hands of God?

Stormie Omartian

A WORD TO THE WISE

The best marriages are built upon mutual trust and a shared faith in God. If your marriage is built upon anything less, then you're building upon a foundation of sand.

VERSE 91

Blessed are those who hunger and thirst for righteousness, because they will be filled.

Matthew 5:6 Holman CSB

LIVING RIGHTEOUSLY

Matthew 5:6 teaches us that righteous men and women are blessed. Do you sincerely desire to be a righteous person? Are you bound and determined—despite the inevitable temptations and distractions of our modern age—to be an example of godly behavior to your family, to your friends, to your coworkers, and to your community? If so, you must obey God's commandments. There are no shortcuts and no loopholes—to be a faithful Christian, you must be an obedient Christian.

You will never become righteous by accident. You must hunger for righteousness, and you must ask God to guide your steps. When you ask Him for guidance, He will give it. So, when you're faced with a difficult choice or a powerful temptation, seek God's counsel and trust the counsel He gives. Invite God into your heart and live according to His commandments. When you do, you will be blessed today, tomorrow, and forever.

MORE THOUGHTS ABOUT DOING WHAT'S RIGHT

Our afflictions are designed not to break us but to bend us toward the eternal and the holy.

Barbara Johnson

Becoming pure is a process of spiritual growth, and taking seriously the confession of sin during prayer time moves that process along, causing us to purge our life of practices that displease God.

Elizabeth George

Holiness has never been the driving force of the majority. It is, however, mandatory for anyone who wants to enter the kingdom.

Elisabeth Elliot

He doesn't need an abundance of words. He doesn't need a dissertation about your life. He just wants your attention. He wants your heart.

Kathy Troccoli

We have a decision to make—to turn away from sin or to be miserable and suffer the consequences of continual disobedience.

Vonette Bright

Impurity is not just a wrong action; impurity is the state of mind and heart and soul which is just the opposite of purity and wholeness.

A. W. Tozer

Righteousness not only defines God, but God defines righteousness.

Bill Hybels

Have your heart right with Christ, and he will visit you often, and so turn weekdays into Sundays, meals into sacraments, homes into temples, and earth into heaven.

C. H. Spurgeon

The great thing is to be found at one's post as a child of God, living each day as though it were our last, but planning as though our world might last a hundred years.

C. S. Lewis

A WORD TO THE WISE

If you really want to follow Jesus, you must walk as He walked—you must strive to lead a righteous life, despite your imperfections.

VERSE 92

*Therefore humble yourselves under
the mighty hand of God, that He may exalt you
in due time, casting all your care upon Him,
for He cares for you.*

1 Peter 5:6-7 NKJV

HE CARES

Of this you can be certain: God is sufficient to meet your needs. Period.

Do the demands of motherhood seem overwhelming at times? If so, you must learn to rely not only upon your own resources, but also upon the promises of your Father in heaven. God will hold your hand and walk with you and your family if you let Him. So even if your circumstances are difficult, trust the Father.

The Psalmist writes, "Weeping may endure for a night, but joy comes in the morning" (Psalm 30:5 NKJV). But when we are suffering, the morning may seem very far away. It is not. God promises that He is "near to those who have a broken heart" (Psalm 34:18 NKJV). When we are troubled, we must turn to Him, and we must encourage our friends and family members to do likewise.

If you are discouraged by the inevitable demands of life here on earth, be mindful of this fact: the loving heart of God is sufficient to meet any challenge . . . including yours.

Snuggle in God's arms. When you are hurting,
when you feel lonely or left out,
let Him cradle you, comfort you, reassure you of
His all-sufficient power and love.

Kay Arthur

MORE THOUGHTS ABOUT GOD'S SUPPORT

God uses our most stumbling, faltering faith-steps as the open door to His doing for us "more than we ask or think."

Catherine Marshall

In God's faithfulness lies eternal security.

Corrie ten Boom

We have ample evidence that the Lord is able to guide. The promises cover every imaginable situation. All we need to do is to take the hand He stretches out.

Elisabeth Elliot

No matter what we are going through, no matter how long the waiting for answers, of one thing we may be sure. God is faithful. He keeps His promises. What He starts, He finishes . . . including His perfect work in us.

Gloria Gaither

A WORD TO THE WISE

If you want God's guidance, ask for it. When you pray for guidance, God will give it.

VERSE 93

In the same way faith,
if it doesn't have works, is dead by itself.

James 2:17 Holman CSB

FAITH WITHOUT WORKS DOESN'T WORK

The central message of James' letter is the need for believers to act upon their beliefs. James' instruction is clear: "faith without works is dead." We are saved by our faith in Christ, but salvation does not signal the end of our earthly responsibilities; it marks the true beginning of our work for the Lord.

If your faith in God is strong, you will find yourself drawn toward God's work. You will serve Him, not just with words or prayers, but also with deeds. Because of your faith, you will feel compelled to do God's work—to do it gladly, faithfully, joyfully, and consistently.

Today, redouble your efforts to do God's bidding here on earth. Never have the needs—or the opportunities—been greater.

It is faith that saves us, not works,
but the faith that saves us
always produces works.

—

C. H. Spurgeon

MORE THOUGHTS ABOUT GOOD WORKS

Where there are no good works, there is no faith. If works and love do not blossom forth, it is not genuine faith, the Gospel has not yet gained a foothold, and Christ is not yet rightly known.

Martin Luther

Those who make religion consist altogether in good works overlook the fact that works themselves are not acceptable to God unless they proceed from faith. For without faith, it is impossible to please Him. And those who make religion consist altogether in faith overlook the fact that true faith always works by love, and invariably produces the works of love.

Charles Finney

No good work is done anywhere without aid from the Father of Lights.

C. S. Lewis

A WORD TO THE WISE

When your good works speak for themselves, don't interrupt.

VERSE 94

So teach us to number our days,
that we may gain a heart of wisdom.

Psalm 90:12 NKJV

THE GIFT OF LIFE

L ife is a glorious gift from God. Treat it that way.

This day, like every other, is filled to the brim with opportunities, challenges, and choices. But, no choice that you make is more important than the choice you make concerning God. Today, you will either place Him at the center of your life—or not—and the consequences of that choice have implications that are both temporal and eternal.

Sometimes, we don't intentionally neglect God; we simply allow ourselves to become overwhelmed with the demands of everyday life. And then, without our even realizing it, we gradually drift away from the One we need most. Thankfully, God never drifts away from us. He remains always present, always steadfast, always loving.

As you begin this day, place God and His Son where they belong: in your head, in your prayers, on your lips, and in your heart. And then, with God as your guide and companion, let the journey begin . . .

MORE THOUGHTS ABOUT LIFE

You have a glorious future in Christ! Live every moment in His power and love.

Vonette Bright

As I contemplate all the sacrifices required in order to live a life that is totally focused on Jesus Christ and His eternal kingdom, the joy seeps out of my heart onto my face in a smile of deep satisfaction.

Anne Graham Lotz

Your life is not a boring stretch of highway. It's a straight line to heaven. And just look at the fields ripening along the way. Look at the tenacity and endurance. Look at the grains of righteousness. You'll have quite a crop at harvest . . . so don't give up!

Joni Eareckson Tada

The world has never been stable. Jesus Himself was born into the cruelest and most unstable of worlds. No, we have babies and keep trusting and living because the Resurrection is true! The Resurrection was not just a one-time event in history; it is a principle built into the very fabric of our beings, a fact reverberating from every cell of creation: Life wins! Life wins!

Gloria Gaither

A life lived without reflection can be very superficial and empty.

Elisabeth Elliot

Jesus wants Life for us, Life with a capital L.

John Eldredge

The value of a life can only be estimated by its relationship to God.

Oswald Chambers

The whole point of this life is the healing of the heart's eye through which God is seen.

St. Augustine

Life is a gift from God, and we must treasure it, protect it, and invest it.

Warren Wiersbe

A WORD TO THE WISE

Your life is a priceless opportunity, a gift of incalculable worth. You should thank God for the gift of life . . . and you should use that gift wisely.

Acquire wisdom—
how much better it is than gold!
And acquire understanding—
it is preferable to silver.

Proverbs 16:16 Holman CSB

ACQUIRING WISDOM

Proverbs 16:16 teaches us that wisdom is more valuable than gold. Do you seek wisdom for yourself and for your family? Of course you do. But as a savvy mom, you know that wisdom can be an elusive commodity in today's troubled world. In a society filled with temptations and distractions, it's easy for parents and children alike to stray far from the source of the ultimate wisdom: God's Holy Word.

When you begin a daily study of God's Word and live according to His commandments, you will become wise . . . in time. But don't expect to open your Bible today and be wise tomorrow. Wisdom is not like a mushroom; it does not spring up overnight. It is, instead, like an oak tree that starts as a tiny acorn, grows into a sapling, and eventually reaches up to the sky, tall and strong.

Today and every day, as a way of understanding God's plan for your life, study His Word and live by it. When you do, you will accumulate a storehouse of wisdom that will enrich your own life and the lives of your family members, your friends, and the world.

Knowledge can be found in books or in school.
Wisdom, on the other hand,
starts with God . . . and ends there.

Marie T. Freeman

MORE THOUGHTS ABOUT WISDOM

If we neglect the Bible, we cannot expect to benefit from the wisdom and direction that result from knowing God's Word.

Vonette Bright

When you and I are related to Jesus Christ, our strength and wisdom and peace and joy and love and hope may run out, but His life rushes in to keep us filled to the brim. We are showered with blessings, not because of anything we have or have not done, but simply because of Him.

Anne Graham Lotz

This is my song through endless ages: Jesus led me all the way.

Fanny Crosby

A WORD TO THE WISE

God makes His wisdom available to you. Your job is to acknowledge, to understand, and (above all) to use that wisdom.

VERSE 96

*And you shall know the truth,
and the truth shall make you free.*
John 8:32 NKJV

TRUTH WITH A CAPITAL T

God is vitally concerned with truth. His Word teaches the truth; His Spirit reveals the truth; His Son leads us to the truth. When we open our hearts to God, and when we allow His Son to rule over our thoughts and our lives, God reveals Himself, and we come to understand the truth about ourselves and the Truth (with a capital T) about God's gift of grace.

The familiar words of John 8:32 remind us that when we come to know God's Truth, we are liberated. Have you been liberated by that Truth? And are you living in accordance with the eternal truths that you find in God's Holy Word? Hopefully so.

Today, as you fulfill the responsibilities that God has placed before you, ask yourself this question: "Do my thoughts and actions bear witness to the ultimate Truth that God has placed in my heart, or am I allowing the pressures of everyday life to overwhelm me?" It's a profound question that deserves an answer . . . now.

We have in Jesus Christ
a perfect example of how to put
God's truth into practice.

—

Bill Bright

MORE THOUGHTS ABOUT TRUTH

Only Jesus Christ is the truth for everyone who has ever been born into the human race, regardless of culture, age, nationality, generation, heritage, gender, color, or language.

Anne Graham Lotz

Those who walk in truth walk in liberty.

Beth Moore

Having truth decay? Brush up on your Bible!

Anonymous

To worship Him in truth means to worship Him honestly, without hypocrisy, standing open and transparent before Him.

Anne Graham Lotz

God will see to it that we understand as much truth as we are willing to obey.

Elisabeth Elliot

A WORD TO THE WISE

You know the importance of the Truth with a capital T. Make sure that your kids know it, too.

VERSE 97

Do not love the world or the things in the world.
If anyone loves the world,
the love of the Father is not in him.

1 John 2:15 NKJV

THE WORLD'S TREASURES OR GOD'S TREASURES?

All of mankind is engaged in a colossal, worldwide treasure hunt. Some folks seek treasure from earthly sources, treasures such as material wealth or public acclaim; others seek God's treasures by making Him the cornerstone of their lives.

What kind of treasure hunter are you? Are you so caught up in the demands of popular society that you sometimes allow the search for worldly treasures to become your primary focus? If so, it's time to reorganize your daily to-do list by placing God in His rightful place: first place.

If you sincerely seek to strengthen your character, you'll focus more intently on God's treasures and less intently on the world's treasures. Don't allow anyone or anything to separate you from your Heavenly Father and His only begotten Son.

Society's priorities are transitory; God's priorities are permanent. The world's treasures are difficult to find and difficult to keep; God's treasures are ever-present and everlasting. Which treasures and whose priorities will you claim as your own? The answer should be obvious.

MORE THOUGHTS ABOUT WORLDLINESS

Our fight is not against any physical enemy; it is against organizations and powers that are spiritual. We must struggle against sin all our lives, but we are assured we will win.

Corrie ten Boom

The more we stuff ourselves with material pleasures, the less we seem to appreciate life.

Barbara Johnson

All those who look to draw their satisfaction from the wells of the world—pleasure, popularity, position, possessions, politics, power, prestige, finances, family, friends, fame, fortune, career, children, church, clubs, sports, sex, success, recognition, reputation, religion, education, entertainment, exercise, honors, health, hobbies—will soon be thirsty again!

Anne Graham Lotz

The true Christian, though he is in revolt against the world's efforts to brainwash him, is no mere rebel for rebellion's sake. He dissents from the world because he knows that it cannot make good on its promises.

A. W. Tozer

As we have by faith said no to sin, so we should by faith say yes to God and set our minds on things above, where Christ is seated in the heavenlies.

Vonette Bright

He who dies with the most toys . . . still dies.

Anonymous

Every day, I find countless opportunities to decide whether I will obey God and demonstrate my love for Him or try to please myself or the world system. God is waiting for my choices.

Bill Bright

A WORD TO THE WISE

Whose message? If you dwell on the world's messages, you're setting yourself up for disaster. If you dwell on God's message, you're setting yourself up for victory.

VERSE 98

For I am the Lord, I do not change.
Malachi 3:6 NKJV

HE DOES NOT CHANGE

Our world is in a state of constant change and so are our families. God is not.

At times, everything around us seems to be changing: our children are growing up, we are growing older, loved ones pass on. Sometimes, the world seems to be trembling beneath our feet. But we can be comforted in the knowledge that our Heavenly Father is the rock that cannot be shaken. His Word promises, "I am the Lord, I do not change."

Every day that we live, we mortals encounter a multitude of changes—some good, some not so good. And on occasion, all of us must endure life-changing personal losses that leave us breathless. When we do, our loving Heavenly Father stands ready to protect us, to comfort us, to guide us, and, in time, to heal us.

Are you facing difficult transitions or unwelcome adjustments? If so, please remember that God is far bigger than any challenge you may face. So, instead of worrying about the shifting sands of life, put your faith in the One who cannot be moved.

Are you anxious about situations that you cannot control? Take your anxieties to God. Are you troubled? Take your troubles to Him. Does your world seem to be changing too fast for its own good? Remember that "Jesus Christ is the same yesterday, today, and forever" (Hebrews 13:8 NKJV). And, rest assured: It is precisely because your Savior does not change that you can face the transitions of life with courage for today and hope for tomorrow.

MORE THOUGHTS ABOUT GOD

God can see clearly no matter how dark or foggy the night is. Trust His Word to guide you safely home.

Lisa Whelchel

We may blunder on for years thinking we know a great deal about Him, and then, perhaps suddenly, we catch a sight of Him as He is revealed in the face of Jesus Christ, and we discover the real God.

Hannah Whitall Smith

To God be the glory, great things He has done; / So loved He the world that He gave us His Son.

Fanny Crosby

God is the beyond in the midst of our life.

Dietrich Bonhoeffer

I lived with Indians who made pots out of clay which they used for cooking. Nobody was interested in the pot. Everybody was interested in what was inside. The same clay taken out of the same riverbed, always made in the same design, nothing special about it. Well, I'm a clay pot, and let me not forget it. But, the excellency of the power is of God and not us.

Elisabeth Elliot

When all else is gone, God is still left. Nothing changes Him.

Hannah Whitall Smith

God does not tell us what He is going to do; He reveals to us who He is.

Oswald Chambers

A WORD TO THE WISE

Because God is infinite and eternal, you cannot comprehend Him. But you can understand your need to praise Him, to love Him, and to obey His Word.

You are the light of the world.
A city that is set on a hill cannot be hidden.
Nor do they light a lamp and put it under a basket,
but on a lampstand, and it gives light to all who are
in the house. Let your light so shine before men,
that they may see your good works
and glorify your Father in heaven.

Matthew 5:14-16 NKJV

Matthew 5 makes it clear taht: you are "the light of the world." The Bible also says that you should live in a way that lets other people understand what it means to be a follower of Jesus.

Your personal testimony is profoundly important, but perhaps because of shyness (or because of the fear of being rebuffed), you've been hesitant to share your experiences. If so, you should start paying less attention to your own insecurities and more attention to the message that God wants you to share with the world.

Corrie ten Boom observed, "There is nothing anybody else can do that can stop God from using us. We can turn everything into a testimony." Her words remind us that when we speak up for God, our actions may speak even more loudly than our words.

When we let other people know the details of our faith, we assume an important responsibility: the responsibility of making certain that our words are reinforced by our actions. When we share our testimonies, we must also be willing to serve as shining examples of righteousness— undeniable examples of the changes that Jesus makes in the lives of those who accept Him as their Savior.

Are you willing to follow in the footsteps of Jesus? If so, you must also be willing to talk about Him. And make no mistake—the time to express your belief in Him is now. You know how He has touched your own heart; help Him do the same for others.

MORE THOUGHTS ABOUT WITNESSING

There is no thrill quite as wonderful as seeing someone else come to trust Christ because I have been faithful in sharing the story of my own faith.

Vonette Bright

We must go out and live among them, manifesting the gentle, loving spirit of our Lord. We need to make friends before we can hope to make converts.

Lottie Moon

If you are going to live in peace, you need to embrace in faith the reality that "the LORD is in His holy temple." Embrace it and be silent before Him. You don't need to argue. You don't need to defend God. Simply explain Him as the Word of God explains Him. Then it is the skeptic's responsibility to accept or reject the Word of God. The responsibility is his, not yours. It's between him and God. It's a matter of faith.

Kay Arthur

God has ordained that others may see the reality of His presence by the illumination our lives shed forth.

Beth Moore

In your desire to share the gospel, you may be the only Jesus someone else will ever meet. Be real and be involved with people.

Barbara Johnson

A WORD TO THE WISE

Whether you realize it or not, you have a profound responsibility to tell as many people as you can about the eternal life that Christ offers to those who believe in Him.

VERSE 100

I was glad when they said unto me,
Let us go into the house of the LORD.
Psalm 122:1 KJV

OUR NEED
TO WORSHIP GOD

All of humanity is engaged in worship. The question is not whether we worship, but what we worship. Wise men and women choose to worship God. When they do, they are blessed with a plentiful harvest of joy, peace, and abundance. Other people choose to distance themselves from God by foolishly worshipping things that are intended to bring personal gratification but not spiritual gratification. Such choices often have tragic consequences.

If we place our love for material possessions above our love for God—or if we yield to the countless temptations of this world—we find ourselves engaged in a struggle between good and evil, a clash between God and Satan. Our responses to these struggles have implications that echo throughout our families and throughout our communities.

How can we ensure that we cast our lot with God? We do so, in part, by the practice of regular, purposeful worship in the company of fellow believers. When we worship God faithfully and fervently, we are blessed. When we fail to worship God, for whatever reason, we forfeit the spiritual gifts that He intends for us.

We must worship our Heavenly Father, not just with our words but also with deeds. We must honor Him, praise Him, and obey Him. As we seek to find purpose and meaning for our lives, we must first seek His purpose and His will. For believers, God comes first. Always first.

Do you place a high value on the practice of worship? Hopefully so. After all, every day provides countless opportunities to put God where He belongs: at the very center of your life. It's up to you to worship God seven days a week; anything less is simply not enough.

MORE THOUGHTS ABOUT WORSHIP

In the sanctuary, we discover beauty: the beauty of His presence.

Kay Arthur

God has promised to give you all of eternity. The least you can do is give Him one day a week in return.

Marie T. Freeman

In Biblical worship you do not find the repetition of a phrase; instead, you find the worshipers rehearsing the character of God and His ways, reminding Him of His faithfulness and His wonderful promises.

Kay Arthur

I am of the opinion that we should not be concerned about working for God until we have learned the meaning and delight of worshipping Him.

A. W. Tozer

God actually delights in and pursues our worship (Proverbs 15:8 & John 4:23).

Shirley Dobson

A WORD TO THE WISE

Teach your kids that worship isn't just for Sunday mornings. Demonstrate to your family that worshipping God is a seven-day-a-week proposition, not a one-day-a-week intermission.

It's helpful to commit key Bible verses to memory. On the pages that follow, jot down your own notes about the verses you intend to memorize.

TIPS FOR MEMORIZING BIBLE VERSES

As you memorize Bible verses, here are some things to consider:

1. It helps to write each verse on a note card and carry it with you throughout the week, reviewing the verse often.

2. Memorization is, at its core, the process of moving things from short-term memory into long-term memory. You achieve this through repetition, which means that the more you recite the verse to yourself, the more quickly you'll learn it.

3. Even after you've memorized a particular verse, it's important to review it again and again throughout the year. Otherwise, a verse you've memorized in January may become little more than a foggy recollection by December.

4. Don't be too hard on yourself. If you can't quite master a particular verse, don't quit and don't lose hope. Instead of berating yourself, just keep reciting the verse over and over, until you finally send it into your long-term memory banks.

_____

_____

_____

_____

_____

_____

_____

_____

_____

_____

_____

_____

_____

_____

_____

_____

_____

_____

_____

_____

_____